SHE JOURNEYS

She Journeys

A Memoir of Heartbreak and Homecoming

Sarah May

SHE WRITES PRESS

Copyright © 2025 Sarah May

Excerpts of Adult Children of Emotionally Immature Parents by Lindsay C. Gibson courtesy of New Harbinger Publications.

Excerpt of The Body Keeps the Score by Bessel van der Kolk courtesy of Penguin Random House.

All rights reserved. No part of this publication may be reproduced, stored in a retrieval system, or transmitted in any form or by any means, electronic, mechanical, photocopying, recording, or otherwise, except for brief quotations in reviews, educational works, or other uses permitted by copyright law.

Published in 2025 by
She Writes Press, an imprint of The Stable Book Group

32 Court Street, Suite 2109
Brooklyn, NY 11201
https://shewritespress.com
Library of Congress Control Number: 2025909820
ISBN: 978-1-64742-962-1
eISBN: 978-1-64742-963-8

Interior Designer: Kiran Spees

Printed in the United States

Names and identifying characteristics have been changed to protect the privacy of certain individuals.

No part of this publication may be used to train generative artificial intelligence (AI) models. The publisher and author reserve all rights related to the use of this content in machine learning.

All company and product names mentioned in this book may be trademarks or registered trademarks of their respective owners. They are used for identification purposes only and do not imply endorsement or affiliation.

To the beautiful people who sheltered me through my darkness.

And to A.,
our love is the best adventure by far.

CONTENTS

PREFACE.................................1

PROLOGUE: THE CALL......................2

PART I: ORIGINS

1: DEPLOYED............................13

2: MONSTERS............................22

3: NEVER SAY NEVER.....................29

4: CRACKS..............................34

5: SHATTERED...........................38

6: REUNION.............................45

PART II: UNDOING

7: SECOND CHANCES......................55

8: THE WIDOWS..........................61

9: UNRAVELING..........................69

10: WAKING UP.................................. 76

11: DARKNESS................................... 83

12: TERROR...................................... 87

13: ENDINGS.................................... 97

14: LEAVING.................................... 104

PART III: HEALING

15: BEGINNINGS............................... 113

16: ROAD TRIP................................. 122

17: THE COMPANY I KEEP..................... 127

18: WORTH...................................... 131

19: STRENGTH.................................. 138

20: BY THE LIGHT OF THE MOON 144

21: A SAFE PLACE 152

22: GOODBYES 159

23: RESPONSIBILITY 165

24: BAND-AID 172

25: TRIGGERED................................. 177

26: INTUITION 183

27: CHOOSING ME.............................. 187

28: FULL CIRCLE 194

29: LINGERING 199

30: RECONCILING 207

31: ABANDONED 215

32: ANCESTORS 223

33: FORGIVENESS 232

34: MEDICINE 239

35: MY BODY IS MY ALLY 247

36: ANSWERED PRAYERS 251

37: THE RITUAL 257

38: THE JOURNEY 262

EPILOGUE 265

A BLESSING 268

SOURCES 270

GRATITUDE 273

PREFACE

To reconcile is to create a bridge between what was and what is. This book was my way of reconciling all that once defined my life, the person *I was* and the decisions I made; wounds that were incurred both as an undeserving victim and as a complicit participant. Healing doesn't have a timeline and trauma doesn't just expire. Time, distance, and recovery have given me the gift of perspective. Rarely in the depths of darkness do we know the lessons she is offering. While this book was written several years after these incidents occurred, the telling is portrayed as it was lived and experienced to the best of my ability. The following events, places, and conversations have been recreated from personal recollection, news articles, journal entries, letters, and interviews with those familiar with the events described. Names and identifying characteristics of individuals and locations have been changed to protect the privacy of those depicted and the chronology of events has sometimes been compressed. Memoir is memory resurrected, and our ghosts may be imperfect. Thank you, dear reader, for crossing this bridge with me.

PROLOGUE
THE CALL

The heart of January on the East Coast has brought a record-breaking cold front—a *polar vortex*, the news calls it. The winter wind stings the lungs with a bone-chilling freeze. Safe and warm in bed, my husband and I are awakened from our slumber by an early morning call.

"I need to head into work early," Nick whispers in the predawn darkness.

"I thought you weren't going to fly today?" I ask.

"I volunteered to take someone's place. One of the crewmen had some pipes burst at his house."

I sleepily watch his silhouette fill the dimly lit closet, my husband of two years—close-cropped jet-black hair and a mustache (at least until I beg him to shave it) contrasts sharply with his fair-skinned face, chocolate-brown eyes, and slightly crooked nose. His tall, lanky frame moves methodically as he pulls out his flight suit and combat boots like he's done countless times before. The military tattoo on his arm ripples as he pulls his shirt on. He disappears into the bathroom to shave the stubble from his chin, my eyes growing heavy.

"Be safe, have a good flight," I mumble when he leans down to kiss me goodbye. Rolling over, I steal a few more moments of sleep before my alarm sounds for work.

I wake to an empty bed. For a brief, beautiful moment between sleep and sunlight, I forget. I forget about the gut-wrenching pain that comes flooding in when I open my eyes fully. With consciousness come memories. Memories that weigh so heavy in my heart I sink further into the mattress. I slowly drag myself from bed and repeat for the hundredth time: *You can't go on like this. It's time to let go.* Maybe today I'll find the strength to tell Nick our marriage is over.

I head to work under a gloomy sky that hangs over a gray city. A glacial chill sweeps the downtown streets. I park in a garage and ride the elevator to the office. From the high-rise where I work at a nonprofit, the views might as well be of a cemetery—everything is cold and lifeless. I shake off my peacoat, hanging it on the back of my chair.

"Hi, hun!" says Cat, my office mate. Her short blonde curls are moussed, and she carries a coffee cup in hand as she smiles from across the room. Like me, Cat is a military wife. Unlike me, she has two children. Cat is witty and unfiltered with expressions like: "They think their shit don't stink," and "Bless their heart," her code for someone as dumb as dirt. I adore her.

"Morning," I say, powering on my monitor. It blinks to life as I open my inbox. With everything going on at home with Nick, I've been withdrawn. My misery must be obvious; graciously, Cat doesn't push.

After two and a half years of schooling to complete my master's, I've landed an entry-level position on the fundraising team. It's my first salaried job, a big girl job. Every day I pack a lunch, dress in business casual, and commute twenty minutes. At twenty-three, it feels supremely more adult than I am. But I love the mission of the organization and my boss, Daryn. Every day she shows up in perfectly coordinated outfits to court donors at lunch or have me attend young professional events with her. The three of us—Daryn, Cat, and I—make a close-knit team, bonded by weekly meetings and the occasional lunch or happy hour.

I click open a Word document to draft a thank-you letter to our most recent donor when a text arrives:

Still flying, baby. I love you so much.

A sharp ache pierces my heart. I believe Nick, but I don't trust him. And the deep, quiet pain that's been a constant for the past several months becomes momentarily staggering. He always texts me when he's flying. No matter what. Our marriage may be ending, but he still says all the right things.

Nick is an aircrewman who flies on one of the military's many helicopters. Practically, he's never gotten the chance to put his training to use and, much to his dismay, probably never will. The war in Afghanistan is ongoing, but all Nick's done for the last few years is train—routine exercises and staged military games for flight hours and signoffs. He'd signed his enlistment papers right out of high school, an idealistic patriot who longed to serve his country. Those days we were just friends. These days my twenty-three-year-old husband complains that his job is frustratingly irrelevant.

The morning hours pass sluggishly as I type away. I jump, startled from a workflow, when my phone vibrates repeatedly on the desk. I don't recognize the number on the screen, but the digits are local. I swipe to answer.

"Hello?"

A female voice fills the other end of the line, "Hi, yes, is this Sarah May?"

I roll my eyes. Probably just another spam call.

"Yes, it is, but I—"

"Sarah," she interrupts, "I'm with the hospital. There's been an incident involving your husband."

My heart catches in my chest.

"Are you nearby?" the woman continues. "It would be best if you can come right away."

My face grows hot. My hands tremble. "What kind of incident? What happened?" The words come out jumbled, demanding. Cat looks over at me.

The woman's voice softens. "Sarah, it's best you come here as soon as possible. Are you able to drive, or is there someone who can drive you?"

There's a buzzing between my ears. I only hear part of what she's said. "What happened? Is he okay?"

She ignores my questions. "Is there someone who can drive you?"

Panic descends at the thought that something has happened to Nick. "I'm fine to drive," I snap. "I'll leave right away. I'm downtown, so I can be there soon." Pleading, I try a final time, "Please, just tell me . . . is he okay?"

"I'm sorry, I can't say more. It's best you come as soon as you can. We'll tell you more when you arrive." She pauses. "He's asking for you, though, so that's a good sign."

I hang up, my stomach knotted with worry. When I rise to stand, my knees shake. From across the room, Cat searches my face with concern, having overheard the conversation. "Do you want me to take you?" she asks.

Already pulling on my coat, I shake my head. "It's okay, but can you tell Daryn I need to leave for an emergency?"

"Of course," she says, but I'm already out the door, running to the elevator.

I tear down the hallway and punch the ground floor button. Every second stretches relentlessly slow. *I just need to be with him.* My only thought, my only concern, is Nick. Nothing else matters. As if waking from a dream, I realize that so much doesn't matter. As I wait, I pray. *Please God, let him be alright . . . please, please, please.* The prayer becomes a mantra of begging. Down the elevator. Through the lobby. The cold stings my lungs as I run on the wet cement. *Please God, let him be okay.*

I reach my car and jam the keys into the ignition, racing toward the hospital on adrenaline. Speeding, I run a red light. My hands tremble at the wheel. *Breathe*, I tell myself, but the panic is spreading. I just need to be with him.

I park at the emergency room and race through the doors. On the other side of the glass, I pause mid-step, stunned. The lobby is filled with news crews. A wave of booms, mics, and cameras greet me. Reporters mill, talking hurriedly. I push through the crowd and give my name to the receptionist.

"Follow me," says the brunette woman behind the counter. We walk around the corner where she opens the door to a private waiting room lined with plastic chairs.

"Please," I implore, "do you know what's going on?"

She shakes her head. "I'm sorry," she says, "but someone will be here to talk with you shortly." She closes the door gently behind her.

I pace with anxiety, my heels *click-click-clicking* on the tile floor. My heart races against my ribs, my mind scrambled. *What happened?* Nick texted me earlier that morning from his flight like he always did. *Why isn't anyone answering my questions?* My frustration grows. *I need answers!* If there are news crews outside, maybe I can find out what's going on. I pull out my phone and search the local news. My eyes quickly scan the breaking headlines.

I freeze.

"No," I whisper. My hand flies to my mouth. Everything stops. My eyes blur as my body wavers.

A helicopter crash.

I collapse back into one of the plastic chairs. My first instinct is denial as I scan the first article:

US MILITARY HELICOPTER CRASH CONFIRMED, RESCUES UNDERWAY

There are already breaking stories on multiple outlets from around the world. BBC. CNN. NBC.

Bodies are missing. Crew members are dead. My husband was on that helicopter.

"Oh my God."

The door opens and the receptionist leads a woman into the room, a wife of one of the other crew members. I stand, quickly embracing her. The words fall out of my mouth with little thought. "Do you know what happened? Did you hear the news?" She shakes her head. I form the dreadful words. "There's been an accident. A crash."

Her turn to panic. "What?!" She exclaims, "Where's my husband?" She wheels around, demanding answers. My own desire is reflected in her stricken face. The receptionist insists someone will come by shortly.

A chaplain enters the room and offers to pray with us. I bow my head as his lips move, but all I hear is a whooshing inside my brain. When he leaves, the other wife and I sit side by side in silence. She places her head in her hands as the minutes tick by.

Eventually, a doctor strides in. "I can take you back now," he says.

We jump up and follow him. Outside the waiting room the throng of reporters has grown. I try to prepare myself, but for what, I don't know. We're ushered through double doors and into the emergency room unit. The other wife spots her husband on a gurney nearby and runs to him. I look up the hallway.

Nick.

He's on the last bed. My feet can't move fast enough as I stumble toward him.

A reflective blanket covers his body, but still, he is shivering. Monitors beep around him. Gauze has been wrapped around his entire skull. His left arm hangs limply in a blue sling. The smoke has charred his face black as tar. His eyes are filled with blood. Open gashes across his face beg for stiches. The sight twists my gut. But he's conscious. He's breathing.

"Nick, baby . . . I'm here." I kneel down by the bed and reach for his hand.

"Sarah," he croaks.

The extent of his injuries paralyzes me. I hear my voice speaking, but the sound is automatic. "Yes, I'm here. I love you so much."

He's having trouble breathing, a half-ragged sound that's taking too much effort. "There was a crash."

"I know," I say, "it's all over the news."

Through disjointed breaths, he tells me what happened. Fire. Impact. Raft. Rescue.

His bloodshot eyes find mine, the whites soaked through in nightmarish red. "I fought for you," he says. "In the water, I prayed. I prayed to survive so I can get my life straight."

My heart swells and I gently squeeze his hand.

"I survived for you, Sarah. For us, for our children."

I nod. We don't have children yet, but I know what he means. He means our future, our forever.

He whispers, "I'm so sorry. God saved me so I could be a better husband. I promise."

I look at the man before me. His face is burned black. His body is broken. But he's alive. It's the only thing that matters.

"It's going to be alright," I say.

He closes his eyes and grimaces.

A doctor arrives to tell us that Nick will be moved upstairs to a private room as soon as his body temperature stabilizes.

"His head?" I ask, motioning to the layers of gauze concealing something ominous.

"Yes, he'll need an operation, but we're working on those in urgent condition first."

However surreal this is, however unimaginable, however nightmarish . . . he's alive. He could have died. He almost *did die*. The same thought rings in my head like the consistent beeps from the monitor. Beep. *I need him.* Beep. *I want him.* Beep. *I love him.*

This changes everything. Today isn't the day I tell my husband our marriage is over. Today is the day we've been given a second chance.

Nothing, not even the affair, can come between us now.

PART I
ORIGINS

1

DEPLOYED

SEVEN MONTHS BEFORE THE CRASH

The night before Nick left for his six-month deployment overseas, we cuddled into the early hours of the morning, trying to stay awake, to squeeze out our last precious moments together. I woke at 3:00 a.m., lights still glowing, his chest rising and falling. My eyes traced his outline, memorizing his face, committing the vision to heart, as if I could keep him preserved.

Melancholic, too sad to speak, we sat at the airport, holding each other tight. When it finally happened, Nick pulled me in close. He brushed a strand of hair behind my ear, his brown eyes glassy as he kissed the top of my head. Lifting my chin and staring intently down at me, he said, "Be strong, baby. Remember, it's us against the world. I love you so much."

Trembling, holding in my own tears, I nodded as we kissed a fierce goodbye. Before I knew it, his airplane had disappeared from sight.

As I walked back into our second-story apartment, happy photos on the walls only heightened my grief and highlighted the sharp aloneness. Home didn't feel like home without Nick. I'd never lived by myself. Growing up with six brothers and one sister, alone was a rare occurrence. And in college, I always had roommates. Closing the door behind me, I uttered a prayer. *Please let these next six months go quickly.*

The next morning greeted me with an empty bed and an emptier heart. Pulling the duvet around me tighter, the untouched pillow beside mine served as a painful reminder. "I miss you already," I whispered to the memory of him. It would be the first of many words spoken to a ghost.

Nick was on the other side of the world. His days were my nights. I knew we could do it, but I hated that we had to. I was a military wife. It was my responsibility to be strong and independent while he was gone. Loneliness was a sacrifice, but I was proud of him, proud of his service. Even if he didn't love his job, he was serving our country. We'd already endured months-long stints apart and shared conversations preparing us for this deployment, the longest one yet. Before he left, he assured me, "We've got this. We've finally grown into the couple we're supposed to be."

Communication and loyalty were our cornerstones for a successful deployment. To minimize any risk, we agreed not to have friends of the opposite gender. Sadly, we knew too many couples whose marriages had floundered in the military, whose spouses had cheated. Thankfully, the challenges of distance weren't new to either of us. After all, Nick and I had fallen in love without ever going on a date. We'd said "I love you" before we'd even kissed.

I was nineteen when our love story began. I returned home that summer after studying abroad in Cyprus and volunteering at a refugee camp in the West Bank. Back in my small California town, nothing had perceptibly changed; but for me, everything felt different. The suffering, the poverty, the blatant injustice. I couldn't forget it. I had one year left before college graduation. Confronted with my privilege, the pressure to decide an uncertain future loomed. I became unglued. Shaken to the core with anger in the face of oppression, yet left reeling with my smallness and insignificance. I wanted someone to understand me, to serve as my anchor in a sea of swirling doubt and the unknown. I was a teenager who wanted to be saved, but being rescued is not the same thing as being loved.

A boy I'd known from high school became my savior. Nick had been a grade below me. We were friends, never more, even though he'd tried. His boyish charm was in his flirtatiousness that extended to seemingly every girl. One-on-one, he was empathetic in a way that made a gal feel seen, heard, special. It was a gift he often used to his advantage. Once, our gaze had met from across the room at a party. He stared with hungry eyes, shameless, undeterred. It didn't matter that I had a boyfriend at the time, didn't matter that I had written off Nick and his pursuits as trivial.

But at nineteen—feeling lost and lonely—I no longer dismissed him. Instead, we reconnected. It started with a phone call where we talked for hours. Stationed across the country, he opened up about his disillusionment with the military. Service wasn't the act of glorified patriotism he'd hoped for. Although we once shared a zip code, our upbringings couldn't have been more different. I was a middle child in a small army of siblings, my parents devoutly religious and loving but limited by marital struggle. Nick was an only child, raised by a single mother whose entire universe centered around him.

On that fateful call, his words became the balm to my loneliness and self-doubt. Somehow, he knew just what to say to ease my pain. All of a sudden, I was the girl he was making feel seen, heard, special. "I've always admired you, Sarah May," he said. Something stirred between us, a curiosity, a desire. That was the first of many phone calls that became our origins. Then, the letters began.

We romantically poured out our hearts, old-fashioned style, with a stamp. Sending each other page after page of our deepest fears and desires. With each envelope, the feelings we had for one another intensified. The letters became filled with admissions of how much we cared for one another. There was the letter that arrived with his dog tag. The letter I sent him tucked into my favorite book. We were swept away by the idea of an *us* without ever going on a date. Over the course of six months, through words penned and lengthy phone calls, we had become *a thing*.

Our relationship hadn't come without challenges. We continued exchanging letters, but on the next call we would fight. Turmoil then bliss, on then off. The only way to see if we could truly work was to be in the same room together.

The opportunity had come over Christmas break my final year of college. Neither of us knew what to expect when I pulled up to his childhood home that winter day. There was so much between us, but at the same time, nothing at all. My hands shook with nervous anticipation as I turned into his driveway. Bracing myself, I parked and took a deep breath. When I looked up, there he was.

He stood outside the doorway, his hands stuffed in gym short pockets, a yellow T-shirt stretched across his torso. A confident smile streaked across his face. His jet-black hair was cut short in a classic military fade. His cheeks flushed from the cold, his brown eyes landed once again on mine. Time seemed to stop.

A world had been created between us. While distance had kept us physically apart, emotionally we had become completely entwined. He knew *everything* about me. I knew *everything* about him. Without a thought, I jumped from the car, pulled by the force of him. The last few feet of distance disappeared as I dove into his arms. Any doubts, any reservations, they all fell away in that embrace.

He picked me up with ease, my head buried into the crook of his neck, heart beating against his chest. "Sarah . . ." he whispered softly in my ear. The wanting beneath his words was palpable. I breathed him in, the smell of Old Spice, his hair still wet from a shower. He was thin, tall, but muscular enough. More than right, somehow, he felt like home. He held me a minute longer. We didn't need to say a word; we'd said it all in our letters and calls.

He released me, his fingers finding mine, pulling me inside. I floated behind him into a den. Beer brands glowed in neon. A worn pool table occupied the center of the room surrounded by dirty leather couches. I feigned interest in a game of billiards, but pool was the last thing on my mind.

Gently, he pushed me up against the table, green suede at the small of my back. I had longed for it, imagined that moment a million times, but when it finally arrived, the surrealness left me reeling. We stood inches apart. Electricity built between us, buzzing like the signs on the walls. All the months of distance and longing had led to this one moment. All our dreaming and desire collided into form.

Nick slowly bent towards me. His lips landed on mine. Gentle, warm, tantalizing. His hands ran down my waist, pulling my body near. The fire built into a wild, untamed inferno that consumed us entirely. He hoisted me up onto the table as I wrapped my legs around him. Shoving pool balls away, he laid me on my back, unbuttoning my jeans. Nothing else mattered. Just him. Just us.

Over that holiday break, we were inseparable. Infatuated kids, too young to buy our own alcohol let alone rent a car or a room at most hotels. Blissfully wrapped up in youth, ignorance, and the sweet naivete of believing we had it all. We became the gushy, over-the-top, roll-your-eyes-at-us kind of couple. He met my massive family and charmed his way into the fold with *mostly* flying colors.

During the following months, we combatted long distance by

texting constantly and talking for hours every day. I drifted away from friends my senior year of college as Nick and I grew closer. When I could, I flew standby to visit him. Our pattern of turmoil then bliss continued—exploding into fights about the smallest things, then making up just as quickly. Impulsive, jealous, demanding all of each other, utterly obsessed with keeping the other happy. It was a gradual descent into making him my everything, but he also made me his. Ours was that kind of relationship. Consuming.

After graduation, I packed up my entire life and moved to the East Coast where Nick was stationed. The wait was finally over. No more stamps. No more lengthy calls. I was headed to graduate school to study conflict resolution and he would continue his enlisted service.

I moved in with him into his military block apartment. Very quickly, *his* life became *our life*. We played like little kids, but made love with passion and intensity. We fought hard, but bounced back stronger. Late at night, holding each other with a desperate need for more, always more, we talked about our future. Even though we were young, we talked about marriage, how many children we wanted, where we would settle down, what kind of home we would have.

Three months after moving in together and a few days shy of my twenty-first birthday, we flew back to California for a family wedding. Adamantly, Nick suggested we visit my favorite gardens at an old estate. Surrounded by thousands of blossoming roses, he released my hand.

"Sarah May . . . ?"

I turned to see him kneeling with a black box in his outstretched hand. A gold ring glittered with diamonds. My vision blurred as my hand flew to my mouth.

"Sarah," he repeated, "you know I love you and want to spend the rest of my life with you. You know that I trust you. I'll never take you for granted, and I'll always work to keep you happy . . . Will you spend the rest of your life with me?"

Swooping down, I embraced him so hard I almost tackled him to the ground. Finding my voice, I uttered the words that would change my life forever. "Yes, yes, yes!"

We exchanged vows five months later, on a perfect day on the California coast. It was crystal clear and temperate, the early morning fog having disappeared with the sun's rays. I walked too fast down the aisle, quaking with nerves, my bare feet sinking into sand, sunshine on my face. A silky strapless dress hugged my body tight. My long blonde hair was meticulously curled and pulled up with white flowers. My gaze was locked on Nick. Not on the aisles of white plastic chairs filled with family and friends or the people gathered on the nearby pier to watch. Not on my sister and bridesmaids or even the dazzling horizon of endless blue. Nothing else existed.

At the altar, my mom rose to join my dad in giving me away. I looked at Nick with anticipation and smiled. We faced each other in front of the officiant, entranced. The beauty of spending an entire life with someone stretched before us, an open book, ours for the writing.

When the officiant offered me the microphone to declare my vows, I accepted with shaky hands, but I'd memorized every word.

"My wonderful Nick, my promise to you is forever. A love never ending, commitment and loyalty undying. My respect, admiration, and appreciation are unwavering. I promise you my friendship through all the years. To always support and encourage the man you are and the man you will be. In difficult times, our faith in God and dedication will see us through. In good times we will treasure and cherish all our blessings. In all we do, all we will go through, I will never stop loving you."

I swear Nick looked at me like I was the only woman in the entire universe. He took the microphone and pulled out a folded piece of paper.

"Sarah May," he read, "my promise to you is forever. My commitment unyielding, unwavering, and undying to our cause. In every day that passes I promise you will know I love you, that you truly are the most beautiful and spectacular woman I will ever know. You will always hold my affection and my gaze, my heart, my passion and desire, my forever and a day. In good times and bad, you will find me nowhere else but by your side."

I wiped away a tear. That was it. When I said, "I do," I gave Nick more than my heart, I gave him my future, my life, all of me. For better or for worse.

He took the ring from his best man and slid it on my finger. *Forever and a day* inscribed on the inside. I did the same, our gold bands glinting in the sun. The rest was a blur: speeches, dancing, champagne, our honeymoon in Hawaii.

We were only a year and a half into our marriage, our *forever and a day*. The only thing between us and the rest of our dreams was this deployment.

My first trip to the grocery store after Nick's departure was overwhelming. Polished tile leered. Bright bulbs felt like an interrogation room. Aisles stretched to infinity. I stood completely stumped in the produce section. *What did I like to eat?* I couldn't remember. *What should I cook for myself?* If the vegetables could speak, they would remind me I used to be a vegetarian. Before Nick. All I could think about was what he would like, what would make him happy. Maybe I was once my own person, but I'd given myself entirely to loving him. Shaking off indecision, I walked each aisle and scanned the shelves, as if they could remind me who I was and what I used to enjoy.

I quickly found the trick to negotiate the chasm my husband's absence left. Stay busy, fill my schedule. It was easy to do. Between my last semester of graduate school, working full-time for a nonprofit, and assisting a wedding planner on weekends, I rarely had a day off. I went to church when I could, but it felt so lonely without Nick that I often skipped service. The weeks passed. Work, eat, exercise, sleep. Repeat. With the fourteen-hour difference, finding time to talk was difficult.

When I missed him most, I imagined our reunion: the magical moment our eyes would meet. Running into open arms. The effortless pickup. Whispering, "Welcome home, baby." Kissing through happy tears. It would arrive before I knew it. At least, that's what I kept telling myself, blissfully unaware.

2

MONSTERS

FOUR MONTHS BEFORE THE CRASH

The familiar Skype tone sounded. I scrambled to answer, and Nick's face filled the screen. Those conversations were my lifeline. We would laugh and flirt; sometimes it escalated into phone sex. Other times we dreamt about our life post-deployment. I smiled into the camera.

"Baby," I chimed, "I'm so happy to see you! How was your day?"

The sour look on his face quickly dissolved my joy. He was stoic, his shoulders slumped, no smile.

"What's wrong? Is everything okay?"

His voice was hard, edgy. "No. Not really . . . it's been a bad day. It's so frustrating out here. The leadership sucks. We never get to fly. There's always something wrong with the helicopters. I'm having a hard time, and I just feel so far away from you. From home. From us."

I tried to be sympathetic with this new normal. We barely talked and when we did there was less connection, more distance. Increasingly pessimistic and withdrawn, Nick rarely asked how I was doing. We ended up having petty arguments where I apologized even though I didn't feel like I should. Frustrated and impatient, I wished he would just snap out of it. *Get over it!* I wanted to say. *You signed up for this!* Instead, I tried to remind him that deployment was temporary. At the end of those few months, we could look forward to spending the rest of our lives together.

∽

I headed into downtown and settled in at my desk. Cat greeted me cheerily, country music playing in the background. We caught up as I took a seat and sorted through a stack of letters—checks waiting to be cashed, donors to be thanked. Fundraising wasn't my dream job, but it was a first step in the right direction.

Helping others had always brought me the greatest joy. I was an idealist who believed that people were good, that individual acts of courage could alter history, and that ultimately, justice would prevail. I was transformed by watching the *Invisible Children* documentary at a high school assembly and mission trips to Mexico, yet life in the rural town where I was raised felt sheltered and small. I set out to make it bigger.

At sixteen years old, with bangs, braces, and acne, I saved every penny from a weekend waitressing job to go to Croatia with my best friend and her family, then set out alone across Europe. Shamelessly, I wheeled a polka-dot carry-on in jelly shoes across Italy, France, Switzerland, and the Czech Republic. Wildly naive and raised Christian, the trip provided me with many important firsts. First time to drink (and subsequently black out when I took one too many shots of absinthe), to dance all night then wander out of clubs at sunrise, to appreciate art, architecture, and history, but most importantly, to open my eyes to the vastness of the world, with all its beauty and brutality, richness and rawness. The experience injected a lust for more.

Three years later, I would study abroad and backpack sans bangs and braces. I lived out of an oversized green pack and navigated with a dog-eared *Lonely Planet* across Egypt, Spain, Morocco, Germany, and Greece. My big sister joined me to travel through Israel and Jordan. Her globe-trotting with Semester at Sea had served as inspiration for my own adventures. Together, we explored Petra by candlelight and Wadi Rum with Bedouins. We lathered each other with mud at the Dead Sea and wandered through Jerusalem's old quarters. I was inexplicably drawn to the Israeli–Palestinian conflict, the history, the complexity, so much so that I would volunteer at a refugee camp. Undeniably, it was my time in the West Bank that had spurred my decision to apply to graduate school and study conflict resolution.

In my dreams, I'd land a job with the United Nations or the State Department or an NGO in the Middle East. In the meantime, I was working my first salaried job in what I hoped would be a meaningful career.

Strange that someone so passionate about peace would end up married to a man in the military. But I knew Nick before he enlisted. And I saw the unhappiness his decision brought him. The military wouldn't be for life. Both of us couldn't wait for the day he got out. Only a few more years and we would never have to be separated for months at a time again.

A few nights later, my Skype sounded again. I muted my new guilty pleasure—*Below Deck*—and hastily ran my hands through my hair. I swiped across the phone screen and Nick's mustached face appeared.

"Hi, babe!" I exclaimed.

"Hey," he greeted me. His jaw was set, his brown eyes downcast as we briefly caught up. He seemed off. Again. Abruptly, he announced, "There's something I need to tell you."

I paused, apprehensive.

"Something happened a while back that I've been feeling really guilty about. I didn't want to tell you sooner because we've been doing so good with the distance."

The words triggered an avalanche of anxiety.

"What happened, Nick?" It came out more demanding than I wanted it to. Silence. I prompted him again, "Whatever it is, you can tell me."

He cleared his throat, avoiding my penetrating stare. "A few months ago," he stammered, "a girl at work saw one of the nude photos I sent you."

"Okay..." *So, she saw it over his shoulder? Not the end of the world...*

"Since she'd already seen it . . . she asked me to send it to her."

My head snapped back, my face crinkling in disgust. *What kind of girl does that knowing he's a married man?*

"So . . . I sent it to her—"

"WHAT?!" My voice was loud, incredulous. I nearly dropped the phone.

"I sent it to her," he repeated. "She'd already seen it . . . so I didn't think it was a big deal . . . but then she said she wanted to know what it would be like to *be with me.*"

I felt like I might throw up.

"That's when I realized I made a mistake. I'm sorry. I just didn't want to tell you sooner because I knew it would upset you."

My brain tried to piece together what he was saying—what he had done—when he had done it. *A few months ago means it would have only been a month into deployment . . . so he's been keeping this from me for two months?* I closed my eyes tight, like I could deflect the information, but it struck old, painful wounds.

"Sarah? Say something," he begged.

"I don't know, Nick. Honestly . . . I'm upset you let that happen . . . but I'm even more hurt that you didn't tell me sooner."

"I know. I messed up. I shouldn't have done it."

"No . . . you shouldn't."

"What can I do?"

I made him wait.

"Honestly, I don't know. We promised each other, Nick. No secrets."

"I know, baby . . . I'm so sorry. I messed up. It was so stupid."

At least he told me. He's sorry. He knows it was wrong. I took another breath. My mantra since getting married sounded in my head: *Pick your battles, Sarah.* I opened my eyes and struggled to find the right words. "Thank you for telling me. I'm really glad you did even though it hurts. We have to be honest with each other, Nick. This is already hard enough as it is."

He still wouldn't meet my gaze.

"I love you. It's going to be alright. We'll get past this. Okay?"

He nodded slowly, but engaged less and less. Feeling him withdraw, I pressed again.

"It was just a mistake. I know you're sorry. I forgive you."

When we hung up, he felt no closer than when the conversation began. A void stretched, more distance than I knew what to do with. I drifted back to reality and finished watching *Below Deck*, but my mind was fully consumed. *The fact that he even told me about the photo was a positive sign, right?* His guilt was an indicator he knew better. Being mad would only push him away. I had to be strong to get *us* through this deployment.

The apartment felt claustrophobic, the couch no longer comfortable. Running away to join a yacht crew of messy millennials and set sail for the Caribbean suddenly sounded rational. A shadow of doubt stirred in my heart. Beneath the promises and vows, underneath the convincing facade of confidence in my husband, something lingered. Fear. The intolerable terror of being hurt again. An intimate knowing that the people we love most in life can wound us the deepest.

My dad had been unfaithful. I'd found out by accident after overhearing my mom talking on the phone to her friend. "Sex addict," she'd whispered, her eyes swollen, face red, shoulders shaking. I had no idea what that meant. I was eleven, maybe twelve. My sister told me they had sat us siblings down before this to break the news, but I had no recollection of that. I just knew, as a small girl who didn't even know how to have sex, that this was bad. The pain in our house squeezed the walls like a vice grip. Betrayal was a monster. Unlike the shadows I thought I saw in the dark, this was the real monster. This beast brought out my mother's rage and triggered my father's shame. Their fights would last hours, if not days.

My siblings and I walked on glass when we came home from school and felt the tension, a telltale sign the storm was imminent. Mom's fits of fury could erupt at anyone for the smallest provocation, the full force of her rampage directed at whoever made the unfortunately timed mistake. The one who couldn't find something in the fridge. The one who hung up the phone when she wasn't done talking. The one who overcooked the pasta. She would scream profanities and insults, her face crimson and contorted. Anger made her unrecognizable. How could I have known the words she screamed were those of her own father? I promised myself I would never be like her. Just as she had probably promised herself she would never be like the man who raised her.

I felt worthless and degraded when the rage was directed at me, awful yet sickeningly relieved when it was someone else. We all knew what to do. It was best to admit fault even if you didn't do anything wrong. Apologize over and over and over until her anger smoldered.

Just like Dad did. "I'm sorry," I heard him say so many times I wondered what it meant.

Shame, unlike rage, is quiet. Yet I heard it just as clearly as my mother's screams. It was whispering at the dinner table when my dad couldn't touch his food. It choked the air around us when checks bounced or bills went unpaid. It spoke the loudest when Mom and Dad sat us down for yet another conversation. "I'm sorry," my dad said with a crestfallen face, "I slipped up." Outwardly, shame didn't petrify the way rage did, but its lingering presence would leave many traces. I promised myself I would never marry a man who would betray me like my dad had betrayed my mom.

I wonder if the pain we're so afraid of becomes a part of us, manifesting in countless known and unknown ways. Does it attract the very thing we most want to avoid? Is this what makes our voices loud and our words mean? Does it lead to cheap hotels booked by the hour to have sex with a stranger while your wife cooks dinner for your eight children at home, worrying about how to pay the bills? I wonder about those children; what they absorb, what they carry, and what they will come to believe about love and marriage.

I didn't yet know that the monsters of my childhood were really just pain in disguise. And that one day, my own pain would be so ugly and frightening that I won't know if I can survive it.

3

NEVER SAY NEVER

THREE MONTHS BEFORE THE CRASH

"Are we still on for lunch today?" Cat asked after I settled in at my desk.

"Definitely, let's head out a little early to avoid the rush," I said as we became engrossed in emails, the morning passing quickly.

Once we ordered our meals, she launched right in. "So, how is the deployment going? How long do y'all have left?"

I sighed. "We're halfway through, so three more months. Overall, it's okay. Some days are better than others. But lately, it's been tough. He's felt more distant. Last week there was a photo situation with a girl he works with . . ."

She raised her eyebrows. I filled her in as she shook her head. When I finished, she stirred her ice tea, considering.

"I hate to even ask this question . . . but are you worried? Deployments are so hard. They can really test relationships."

Her question took me back. To the times when Nick and I *had* kept our secrets and the cost of their keeping.

I responded, "We've had our share of difficulties, but they're behind us now. To be honest, we both made mistakes when we were dating."

"Really?"

I sighed heavily as the memories resurfaced.

"Nick and I had been dating a few months long-distance . . . This was after that Christmas we were together for the first time," I explained. "One night at a party I drank too much. There was a guy. We kissed in a swimming pool. Nothing else happened, but I called Nick the next day. I was hungover and heartsick. I told him about it right away. Sobbing, I told him how sorry I was, how stupid it was. I thought it was over between us, that I had sabotaged the best thing to ever happen to me. But his response was so strange. He kept saying over and over, 'Just please don't leave me, Sarah. Don't leave me.' I thought, shouldn't I be the one saying that? Soon, I would know why."

Cat cocked her head, listening intently.

"A few weeks later, he had his own confession. He called, hysterical, and asked how I had the courage to be honest . . . He'd been keeping his own secrets for months. He'd slept with two other people. One of them his high school ex. He was sorry, he'd do anything to earn back my trust. Could I ever forgive him?"

She groaned. I paused.

Sadness crept into my voice as I remembered the devastation of his admission. The way I told him I needed to think before hanging up the phone and staring out my dorm room window where palm trees danced in the Southern California breeze.

I had taken a pillow and held it to my face, letting the anger that was choking me come out with a horrendous scream. Yes, I'd kissed someone else, but it felt small in comparison. I'd crossed a line, but hadn't trampled over it completely. I'd confessed right away, while he'd kept it a secret for months. Was there righteousness to be found in whose treachery was worse? When I'd run out of air, I punched the pillow with all the force my body could manage. When the anger dissolved to sadness, the punching turned to whimpering, my body collapsed on top of the pillow. We were just kids who'd got drunk and made mistakes while trying to have a long-distance relationship. We were hopelessly and helplessly in love. He was sorry. He would do anything to fix it. Of course it hurt, but not as much as the thought of losing him.

It had been a simple decision. Choosing his love was worth it. For some, what had happened would have been a non-negotiable. But a relationship can survive indiscretion; some can even thrive in its wake. I'd seen it myself. In the scorched earth of my parents' marriage, they had eventually planted and nourished a garden, a redeemed love of grace and forgiveness. They overcame it all to grow old together.

In the aftermath, Nick swore, "I would rather die than hurt you like that ever again." We both knew how it felt to be cheated on and what was at stake. We wouldn't compromise us, we agreed. *Never again*. I had called Nick back.

"I forgive you," I'd said, "we can make this work."

I looked across at Cat who could tell this wasn't easy for me to share. "Oh, honey . . . I'm so sorry. I had no idea."

I nodded. "Thank you. It took a lot for us to get past it, but we did. When we got married, we put those mistakes behind us. We've come a long way."

She placed her napkin on the table and paused a moment. "I'm so glad to hear it. But I'm just curious . . . what would you do if it happened again . . . if he cheated?"

I sat my lemonade down, the question weighing heavy. In truth, it was my deepest fear. "He wouldn't do that to me. Not again. It almost destroyed us. But . . . if he did, I don't think I could get past it. I could never forgive him."

She smiled kindly from across the table. "In my experience, we just can't know what we would do until we're in that situation. I've learned to never say never."

She meant well, but her words stung. Conversation finished, we got the check and headed back to the office. The rest of the afternoon I couldn't focus. My mind elsewhere, across the sea, around the world. *Was Nick hanging out with photo girl? Would he steer clear of her like he promised?*

I consoled myself with memories of how we'd repaired before.

After he'd confessed back in college, I had flown to visit him as soon as I could. We hadn't seen each other in months and the indiscretions had taken their toll. We were both miserable, emotionally wracked by guilt, offering contrite apologies and assurances as we tried to rebuild trust.

Outside the airport, he'd been waiting next to his lifted truck, an oversize bouquet of red roses in his hands. He picked me up when I ran to him and held me tight. "You deserve them," he'd said, pressing the flowers into my arms. Driving back to his apartment, he had one hand on the wheel, the other hot on my thigh.

He'd kept that hand on me at all times, even as he carried my bags into his apartment and closed the door. I'd turned to see the glow of candles and a pathway of rose petals. Scattered across the bed were handwritten notes of all the things he loved about me. I started to cry. His hands ran across my waist as he pulled me back into him. "I'm sorry," we'd both said, kissing through tears. "I love you," we'd said over and over as he pulled off my silk blouse, unzipped my boots, and peeled off my leggings. As he lowered me onto the bed and looked at me with eyes that said, *There's only you*. As I lost myself in him. For all Nick's excess, for all our faults, his love was an oasis in the desert of my hurt. I drank it up. I knew I was right to forgive him. To try and make us work. I knew we were worth it.

Later that night a thunderstorm rolled in. He opened the window and let the humid air pour over us. Lying awake, naked, blissful, tangled up. His fingers traced across my body, counting the freckles splashed across my skin. "I want to memorize every inch of you," he said.

"No need," I said. "You'll have me forever, baby. Forever and a day."

I cling to that memory for comfort. The romance, the passion, our vows to one another on our wedding day. That was Nick, that was us.

Still, I can't help but replay Cat's words. They echo in my head, creeping in the darkness, lying in wait. *Never say never.*

4
CRACKS
TWO MONTHS BEFORE THE CRASH

Over the next few weeks of deployment, Nick went out partying more and more. Our calls became infrequent and the distance between us seemed to grow. I hated being at home without him, wondering who he was with and what he was doing. *Was photo girl around? Was Nick drinking too much?* A sick feeling grew in the pit of my stomach day by day.

"You're being so insecure," he would tell me when I raised my concerns the few moments we did talk. It was true, but I also knew how he could be when he drank. When Nick let loose, he was wild, impulsive, the life of the party who just wanted to keep the party going. A day without speaking turned into two, then three. He was busy, he said. Still pained by his secret about photo girl, I wanted reassurance, but any conversation about his behavior quickly escalated into a fight. I could feel it in the stretches between our conversations; we were on a slippery slope into dangerous territory. A dance with the darkness begins in the shadows.

The fear became a daily presence. It greeted me in the morning, sitting on the edge of my bed before work. As I rose and dressed, it taunted me. As I worked out, made dinner, and showered, it haunted me. Cracks began to appear, little fissures in what I thought was solid ground beneath my feet. And on a cold, dreary day in November, the fissure split wide open.

I stared at Nick's face through the phone screen, seething. I was propped up on a hotel bed attending my last weekend course of graduate school. My eyes were daggers, my face hot. After the photo incident, he'd agreed to steer clear of her. Now, he was backtracking. She was just a friend; *I* was the one being dramatic.

"You're being crazy," he snapped. Calling a woman crazy is like cutting the little red wire on a bomb . . . It's the wrong damn one.

My voice shook. "Are you serious? You promised. We both agreed, *Nick*." I spat his name aggressively. I wanted him to feel my anger.

He lashed back. "You're overreacting because you're on your period and all hormonal and shit, *Sarah*."

Bomb detonated.

"You're joking, right?" I shook my head, snorting with indignation, my voice rising. "We both agreed to not have friends of the opposite sex! You said it yourself before deployment, it's a risk we don't need to take. It compromises us!"

I tried to reason, to remind him, but it was useless. Unquestionably, if the tables had been turned, Nick would be livid.

"She understands me," he retorted. "You could never understand what it's like out here." I cringed as he continued, "She's been here for me when you haven't been. Honestly, she's really broken and needs a friend. In a lot of ways, she reminds me of my mom."

I felt queasy, hot with disgust. I couldn't decide which was worse: that he sent a nude photo to a woman who reminded him of his mother or the accusation that I hadn't been there for him. It was too much. Through the nearsightedness of anger, I felt incapable of reaching him. The only power I had was whether or not we spoke. I grasped for a semblance of control that slipped through my fingertips like sand. *Maybe silence will wake him up? Give him a hard reminder of what he's risking?*

"I don't think we should speak for a while," I said coldly. "I want you to understand how serious this is. You're jeopardizing us, our marriage, everything we've worked so hard for." I paused, letting my words sink in. "Call me when you want to act like my husband again. I love you, Nick, but you need to wake up."

I hung up, sounding stronger than I felt. Sweat pricked my arms. My breath was rapid and shallow, the only sounds in the quiet room. *How was this happening?*

I tried to recall the last time he and I had been on solid ground, searching desperately for evidence that not long ago, we had been good, great even. Truthfully, the entire deployment had been hard. The last genuine happiness I remember is from before he left. *Right?*

In the days leading up to his departure, I had spared no expense to maximize our time together. There was a Jet Ski ride to a pod of dolphins, lobster at our favorite restaurant on the water, a photoshoot at the nearby botanical gardens. But on one of our final nights together, we got in a fight. It might have been one of the stupidest arguments we'd ever had. All over a plate of nachos.

"Why are you like this? I just want to help. But you're so controlling," he'd huffed when I told him I wanted to microwave the plate of chips and cheese by myself.

"I just know how I like them, Nick. That's all. It's not that big of a deal." It was so trivial, so silly.

"You always do this. I want to do something nice for you, but you get so crazy about everything. I don't know why I even bother."

I became defensive. *It's just a plate of fucking nachos*, I wanted to say. But I also felt a creeping, familiar feeling. Maybe I *was* controlling.

It came back to this in our fights so many times. I apologized. I said sorry over and over again until he let it go. Just like I'd done with my mom. I needed us to be okay. I would sacrifice so much on the altar of okay. After all, Nick would be leaving soon.

But the inconsequential things we argued about were actually smoke screens for something much bigger. Truths we preferred to dance around, too terrified to name what we secretly feared the most. What if it had always been about trust? After all, control is the mechanism to try and manage what we don't have faith in.

I came back to my senses in that cold, lifeless hotel room. The terrifying prospect of my husband getting close to another woman wedged itself like an ice pick in my chest. It made me panic. The panic turned to anger. I hated the powerlessness. I hated photo girl. I hated that Nick was willingly slipping away and I felt helpless to reach him.

Like unstoppable waves and their inevitable erosion of the shoreline, there was a consistent and steady decline of all that I thought was once proud, stable, and strong between us. The fractures in our foundation cracked my heart with fear, but the nightmare had only just begun.

5
SHATTERED
FIVE WEEKS BEFORE THE CRASH

I sat on the edge of our bed, holding the phone to my ear, gripping the sheets with my left hand, trying to cling to something, anything. The gold of my wedding ring glinted up at me, catching my attention, as if she too was wondering what her future held. It was predawn, and our bedroom was dark, save for the lamp next to the bed. Next to the light sat one of my favorite wedding photos of Nick holding me in his arms. We stood on a sea cliff, the ocean dazzling behind us; there were smiles on our faces and adoration in our eyes. I drew in a sharp breath. There was silence on the other end of the line.

"Did you?" I asked quietly.

No response. I mustered the nerve and asked again, but I already knew the answer. Even though we had less than two weeks left in the deployment, it had been dancing on the edges of my undoing. Hints had been made; red flags raised. Like when he said he no longer felt the spark between us or how he made a list of the pros and cons of being married. The past few weeks we'd barely spoken, and when we did, he was distant. The silent treatment had backfired. I'd foolishly hoped it would bring him around. Instead, he'd run into the open arms of photo girl.

The irony was that at the beginning of this deployment, one night he'd broken down crying and said, "Sometimes I worry that you'll go to someone else. That you'll want someone who can always be there for you and give you everything." All along, he'd been projecting his monster on me. I wrapped the sheet tighter in my hand.

"Did you cheat on me, Nick?"

The quiet stretched. I waited, my heart braced with dread. Desperately, I prayed that I was wrong.

Finally, he broke the strained silence.

"Yes."

I slumped forward, my eyes shut tight against his confession. The ground beneath me gave way and I free-fell. It had all been conjecture. I had known, but didn't want to believe. I had seen, but didn't want to look. The fear in the pit of my stomach, the dark voice whispering in the back of my mind. It had been there for months. Somehow, his confirmation was still a shock. "How?" I choked out. "How could you do this?"

More silence filled the line.

"You said you would rather die than hurt me again."

"I know," he said flatly. No explanation, no emotion.

Why isn't he saying more? Why isn't he apologizing or freaking out or breaking down like last time? Anger—hot and raw—surfaced. I tried again. "How could you?!"

Our wedding photo mocked me from the corner of my eye. Disgusted, I grabbed it and threw it across the room.

"What was that?" he demanded.

"Nothing," I said with a shaky voice. Even then, I couldn't admit I'd thrown it. "How long?" I demanded.

"I took off my wedding ring last week . . ." His voice was distant, removed. "She's in love with me . . ." he trailed off.

I keeled over from the stabbing sensation in my chest. This wasn't just sex; it was something else, something more. Bile rose in my throat, acid on my tongue. I didn't want to ask, but I heard my voice quivering. "Do you love her?"

My entire body tensed, waiting for the final axe.

"I don't know," he said. "I'm confused."

Everything crashed down around me.

"I'm sorry," he finally offered. An empty afterthought.

He didn't sound sorry. He didn't sound like he cared. He didn't cry, didn't get angry. The only glimpse of emotion was the sharp question when I threw our wedding photo. Other than that, there was nothing. No regret. No remorse. Nothing at all.

I hung up and sat rigid. Staring, but not seeing; breathing, but with no life. My thoughts moved through quicksand. The heaviness in my bones dragged me to the floor, where I kept sinking. Downward, depthless. A foggy voice in my brain told me it couldn't be true. It wasn't happening; it was just a bad dream. But my body responded with despair; she knew the truth, she felt it. The blow struck my gut with a crippling ache.

I rose numbly from our bed. The sun had risen, melting the ice crystals that clung to the grass outside. I walked to the living room and lay on the floor where I texted my boss, Daryn:

I'm so sorry, but I woke up sick this morning. I won't be able to come into work today.

In the apartment Nick and I had made into a home, surrounded by all things us, I spiraled. Immobilized, I curled up on the carpet in the fetal position. Tears fell with such ferocity my eyesight blurred as the floor dampened around me. Sobs turned to heaving as the panic spread.

I couldn't stop thinking about them together. His hands running down her waist like they used to run down mine. His lips on hers. He knew it was wrong, but he wanted her so badly that he didn't care. The moment he crossed the line, did he think of me? Did he stop and consider, even briefly, all that he was throwing away? I felt like I was suffocating, hands clamped tight around my throat, choking me until I lost consciousness in a void of pain.

Big shocker, Sarah, the man who cheated before marriage cheated during too. The silly thing is, I believed him. In that room surrounded by rose petals and candles and sweet notes, I forgave him. I trusted him when he said, "Never again." I was so confident on our wedding day, so sure he'd meant his vows to me. The truth was made so much more painful when I realized I'd been complicit in the deception, in keeping the pretense of what I wanted to be true, even though I'd been given all the contrary evidence.

The agony was searing, blinding, incapacitating. *I wasn't enough.* I had been rejected, humiliated, abandoned. The rug of my world had been pulled out from under me. Our vows, our dreams, my forever. A dark thought skirted the fringes of my brain: *You don't have to feel this.* He'd chosen someone else. Her over me. I'd tried so hard to be the perfect wife. I'd done everything for Nick. I'd given all of myself to him, to our relationship, and now, I had nothing left. I didn't want to live with it. *I couldn't.* The voice from the shadows of my mind grew louder: *There's another way, a way that you can disappear.* I felt reckless, obliterated, desperate to end the nightmare. Anything to escape the life that was collapsing before me.

Pulling myself up from the carpet, I wiped my eyes, then padded into our bedroom and rummaged under our bed. Nick was a gun enthusiast and, over time, we'd accumulated a small arsenal of semi-automatic firearms that were stowed under the bed. My fingers found what they sought as I pulled out the gun case.

Click. The plastic latches popped open. A pistol sat inside, already loaded. I slowly removed it with shaking hands, the cold metal harsh against my skin.

I walked back to the living room. Gun in hand, bullet at the ready. I lay on the floor. Pain can make us unpredictable, rash, desperate. I wanted to vanish. I didn't want there to be a tomorrow if it felt like this. I'd lost everything. My husband, my best friend, my future, my life.

I undid the safety.

Nick called sometime later. I was still on the floor, unable to move, panic rising then subsiding, consuming then regressing. The gun lay next to me.

"I can't do this," I told him through hysterical sobs. "I don't want to live. It hurts too much."

"Sarah," he said pleadingly, "try to breathe."

He stayed on the phone until I was consolable, until the hyperventilating receded, until I promised I wouldn't pull the trigger. It gave me some hope that he still cared.

Before we hung up, he said quietly, "This isn't fair."

I didn't understand what he meant. But afterward, I wondered, *Did I mean it? Could I really have pulled the trigger?* I'd threatened my own life, making him responsible for my pain, but also making him my salvation. I made myself sicker with the idea that he was my world and without him I had nothing. I was nothing.

Five days after the discovery, I felt constantly nauseous even though I'd barely eaten. I went to work numb and came home lifeless. Unable to sleep, I had no energy. All I wanted to do was stop the ceaseless visions that filled my brain of my husband loving another woman.

I wanted Nick to understand my hurt, for his world to be eviscerated like mine had. I wanted to see him break because so far, he'd shown nothing—no regret, no sincere apology, no willingness to end the affair. He would be coming home in a little over a week, and no matter what I did, I was torn in two.

Life existed on a spectrum. One minute I hated him with a blinding rage and the next I desperately longed for him. One minute I was so disgusted by him that I never wanted to see him again and the next I couldn't wait until that moment. One minute I didn't know if we could be together and the next I couldn't imagine life without him. I thought about leaving: Where would I go? What would I do? At twenty-three, I still had my whole life before me . . . just a radically different one than I had planned. *I could move to Europe and work for the United Nations. Maybe I'll get a dog. I can hike the Pacific Crest Trail. I could audition for Below Deck.*

What if it had always been so hard for Nick and me because we were simply not right? But what if all that happened could make our marriage stronger? Maybe we could be like my parents. They'd made strides. My mother no longer raged; my father no longer relapsed. They were the happiest they had ever been. They faced the darkness within each other and the shadows within themselves. They were living proof that rebuilding after obliteration was brave, that the worst thing to happen to them led to the very best version of them. *If their marriage survived the unimaginable, maybe ours could too.*

I learned from a therapist's book about infidelity that affairs usually don't last. What was once sexy and irresistible in the dark of night eventually gets exposed in the light of day and the passion fades. I told myself that he had been swept away by infatuation, that what he shared with photo girl wasn't real. Perhaps it was blind faith, or pure illusion, but I knew he still loved me. And I still loved him. For the boy in high school who pursued me, the enlisted soldier who'd written letter after letter dreaming of a life together, the romantic who had made grand gestures and left love notes all over the house, the man who said his vows and promised forever, but mostly, for who I knew he was capable of being. I didn't want to leave that version of Nick. Not yet. I couldn't. I was willing to wait, to try. Because when you love someone so much, when you believe in something like *us* so much, confronting the agony of betrayal is better than a life without them.

Maybe when I held him again it would break the spell of delusion. Being together could remind him. Before I flew to be with my family for Christmas, I left him a note.

> *Dear Nick, I'm sure it feels strange to be home, surreal. I can't really imagine what you are feeling, but I'm glad you're finally here. You can be reminded of who and what we are. Everything is going to be different. We can fix us, save us. I've tried to show you I love you as much as I possibly could. I will always love you. We will get through this. I can't wait to see you.*

It would be waiting for him at home. For months, we'd planned this gathering. I would spend time with my family, then he would join us for the holiday once he returned from deployment.

I traded my dream reunion for a desperate one: Nick would walk through the door and drop his bag. He would see the note on the kitchen counter and our wedding photos on the wall. He would sleep in the bed we shared, feel the traces of me. He'd read my words, and his heart would start to question: *What have I done?*

6

REUNION

THREE WEEKS BEFORE THE CRASH

Sitting in the airport arrivals terminal, I watched people reunite. Loved ones waiting with flowers, signs, smiles, and open arms. I had none of that. Sometimes it hurt so bad, I had to look away. My body was tight as a coil, my feet tapping anxiously, arms crossed. The two-hour drive from the mountain cabin my family had gathered at for the holiday was full of nerve-racking what-ifs. I had dreamt of a Hallmark reunion for so long, the running leap into open arms, the tears of happiness, that first kiss after months of separation. But now, instead of hugging Nick, I wanted to hit him. Instead of joy, I felt only suspended dread. I tried to prepare myself while I waited for what felt like the longest hour of my life.

His form eventually appeared on the walkway. In spite of the pain, my heart still leapt at the sight of him. I spotted him before he saw me. His brown eyes scanned the waiting faces. Then, our eyes met. There was no smile from either of us, but so much felt spoken in the seconds he walked toward me.

Suddenly, we were face-to-face. His arms wrapped around me. I stood on tiptoes in my black boots to reach around his neck. I was so many things: heartbroken and overjoyed, angry and hopeful, weak and loving. He was familiar. He was home.

He whispered into my neck, "I forgot how little you are." The closeness of him. The realness of him. His warmth, his smell. Even then, it hurt, but I knew I loved him. I'd never stopped.

Like strangers, we were awkward. Neither of us spoke as we waited at baggage claim. The airline had lost his luggage. We filed a claim, but he was frustrated, short-tempered.

"Damnit!" he muttered under his breath. "I shouldn't have come. I knew this was a mistake."

I observed him silently, as if from a distance. I was afraid to be myself around him; my grief was a weakness he could exploit. The long drive stretched before us. It offered some of the only alone time we would have over the next week as we shared Christmas with my family.

As we merged onto the freeway, Nick was silent, still fuming about the lost luggage. I gazed ahead, my body angled away from him as if to protect myself. *Was he going to say anything?*

Like they had a million times since the confession, images of Nick and photo girl together burst into my mind, unbidden. Photo girl's hands are on him, pulling off his clothes as he pushes her down onto the bed. She is saying his name. His lips are on her body. My hands shook with rage. The anger built, the images were incessant, and they pushed me over a ledge. I could no longer contain myself. I exploded.

"I'm so mad at you. You said our mistakes were behind us!"

Hitting traffic, the car slowed to a crawl, a line of red taillights before us.

I hissed, "You made a vow, Nick, and you broke it. You betrayed me. You betrayed our marriage. You betrayed yourself. You've been so selfish. This entire deployment, I stayed strong and did my best.

But you . . . you make me sick. I would never, *ever* have done that to you."

He snapped, cutting off my verbal torrent. "You want to know the truth?" he said. "It's your behavior that earned you this affair."

"*My* behavior?" I sputtered. "Are you serious?"

We engaged in a back-and-forth as our voices rose until we were shouting. Outside, a light snow was falling, big flakes smattering across the windshield. The serene landscape couldn't have been more at odds with the inferno raging inside the car. I was so mad about everything that I was mad I was crying.

He finished the conversation with a sharp stab. "Maybe I've just fallen out of love with you."

At that, I shattered, at a loss for what to say to the stranger beside me. We continued up the winding roads in silence, carrying us away from what I had hoped would be an apologetic reunion. That rosy fantasy was a distant dream, a reality replaced with nothing but thorns.

Back at the cabin everyone embraced him. I forced a smile, but I wondered how no one saw right through me. Aside from Mom and Dad, no one had any idea about his indiscretion. I hadn't told anyone else in the family—to protect us, to protect him. I knew that if I'd shared our secret, he wouldn't have come, barricaded by shame. I needed him to be there, to help remind him of the family he was a part of. I pretended around the people who knew me best, fooling them, unable to deceive myself.

When we made it downstairs to our designated bedroom, my shoulders slumped, exhausted from the effort of pretending everything was okay. I took a hot shower, the scalding water washing away the words from earlier. My hair dripping wet, I toweled off and slipped into my pajamas.

Emerging from the bathroom, I stood by the bed, where Nick pulled me in close. Tracing his fingers across my cheek, his eyes—simultaneously wanting and resentful—asked a question. He tilted my head toward his, his mustache brushing against my skin. His lips found mine. Our first kiss after so long. After so much. He was soft, warm, familiar.

Somehow, anger dissolved into desire, rage into passion. I had hurt so badly for him, for us. I answered his question as I kissed him back. I was hungry. Starving for love, for a positive sign from him, for his attention and affection. Sex had always made everything better between us. I hated that I gave in so easily, but more than anything, I wanted him, all of him. *Could this remind him of our passion?* I gave in. I melted into him as he disappeared into me.

Over the next few days, Nick and I became reacquainted. His luggage arrived like a sign that things could be okay. We would snowboard all day then sit in the jacuzzi as snow fell, talking and joking with my siblings. We somehow convinced my parents to play beer pong, where my mom dominated the table, then laughed till we cried playing Cards Against Humanity. Nick and I even performed "What Does the Fox Say?" for the annual family lip-sync competition—an outrageous spectacle where everyone dresses up, with choreographed moves and outfits to match.

Just as nature has her seasons, so too had my family. The winters had been hard, but they never lasted. In the light of the sun, there was an abundance of laughter, fun, and rarely a dull moment. Dance parties in the living room, family movie nights, bonfires with friends, nightly dinners where everyone shared the best and worst parts of their day. And love. Nick was a part of all of that now. This wild family of mine had accepted him like a son, like a brother.

Hope came in flashes, when things felt like they used to with him. His charm, the way he touched me, a look from across the room. Then, just as quickly, a switch flipped, he would disappear, and a new man would take his place. This other man was cold, selfish, uncaring. We were reunited, but still separated by so much.

He continued to text with photo girl. Disappearing for stretches, then returning as if nothing had transpired. Already insecure, it made me crazy. In my desperation, I would read the texts when he left the room. He made no effort to delete them, even after I confronted him. They still said, "I love you." She thought he would leave me to be with her. She reminded him, "I'm waiting for you."

When I saw their words, a rage took over. I had violent daydreams about hurting her; getting some sick satisfaction from her pain consumed me. What must she feel? Was she sitting triumphant, gloating? I hated this woman. I hated her with a fiery fury that made my hands shake, my body grow hot, and my breathing rapid. I was too blinded by the consuming fire, all directed at her, to save enough for Nick. He got the red-hot embers, but she would be burned at the stake. The violence in my head terrified me.

When I initiated a conversation with Nick about us, he was ambivalent. "I don't know what I want. I'm really confused right now," he would say.

A few nights into the trip, I woke to the glow of his phone as he tapped away at the screen. My eyes focused and registered, snapped wide awake by the content. I froze. Nude pictures of photo girl on his screen followed by an explicit, graphic exchange of what they would do to one another. Right next to me, in the same bed where we'd had sex earlier, with my entire family sleeping upstairs.

"What do you think you're doing?" I demanded.

"What?" he said nonchalantly, angling his phone away so I could no longer see the screen.

"Seriously? I'm lying right next to you . . . How can you say, 'What?' You're killing me, Nick. You're fucking killing me."

I turned my back to him. I wished I was strong enough to get up and leave right then and there. That I would have had the self-respect to demand decency. I wished that I could shake him so hard that his bones would remember who he used to be and how he used to love me. But I didn't. I just lay there, crying in the dark, not yet grasping that the battle I was fighting was unwinnable. That I was scrapping all alone. That this new Nick didn't care enough to step into the ring, let alone give us a chance. I wish I could say I loved myself enough to know what I deserved, but the sad truth is, in that moment, I still loved him more than I loved me. And that, *that*, would be my undoing.

Nick and I returned home after a week with my family. Snow fell outside, blanketing everything in soft white. The willow trees outside the apartment were naked. The creek that flowed through the complex was frozen over. A cold apartment waited, but a colder marriage filled the once-happy space. I asked him to go to therapy, to read a book about overcoming the affair, but he wouldn't commit. He begrudgingly went to counseling, sitting impassively. In my wretched attempts to remind him of our passion, we continued to have sex. I pushed away the images that bombarded my brain as his body collided into mine.

New Year's was spent with my friend Lori and her family. Lori knew we were struggling, but it wasn't until that night that she met Nick for the first time. She watched us closely, picking up on the ever-present tension. She pulled me into the kitchen, her eyes filled with concern.

"Why is he acting like nothing is wrong? He's being so fake, Sarah. I guess I expected something else... *someone* else. Is he even the least bit sorry?"

No. No, he's not, is what I wanted to say. Instead, I shrugged. "We're trying to make it work." She shook her head sadly, her eyes telling me what I already knew: *You deserve better.*

I returned to work, despondent and increasingly depressed. I went through the required motions, day after day, but it seemed Nick never really came back from deployment. When the military plane had disappeared, it had taken the man I'd known. Our marriage had been dead for longer than I could admit. Still, the thought of ending it crushed me.

Before I turned off the light for another night of tortured sleep, I glanced at Nick. He was on his phone again, the glow illuminating his face as he tapped away. An invisible barrier separated us, and even though we still shared a bed, we shared little else. I turned off the light and thought about my new tattoo.

Before Nick had arrived for Christmas, an artist had painted the length of my foot with a vibrant phoenix feather. It served as my reminder to rise, to ascend from the ashes when everything crumbled. But as the ink settled, I realized that when a world burns, the fire takes everything along with it, that death is the toll for transformation.

In the dark, I grieved for my marriage and all that was lost. I grieved for the life I had planned on living with him. I grieved because I knew it was over between us and the time had come to say goodbye. "Forever and a day" was nothing but pretty words for an empty promise.

Tomorrow, perhaps, I would find the strength to tell my husband our marriage was over.

PART II
UNDOING

7

SECOND CHANCES
DAY OF THE CRASH

When Nick's body temperature stabilizes, a nurse wheels him to various tests, then moves him upstairs into a private room. A large window overlooks a dreary parking lot. A single recliner sits next to the hospital bed. The walls are covered in beige paint, a small television hangs in the corner, linoleum flooring shines aggressively from the fluorescent lights above.

I sit next to the hospital bed, holding Nick's bandaged hand. Looking at his blackened face and bloodshot eyes, I try to adjust to his appearance, but the sight is startling. When the flurry of nurses and doctors subsides and we have a moment to ourselves, he tells me the full story of what had happened on the helicopter that morning. A story that no one, not the news channels, and not even the military had heard yet.

Soaring above the Atlantic, miles off the coast, the flight was only a few hours underway when an explosion erupted over his shoulder. "Smoke and flames in the cabin!" someone shouted into the headset. Within seconds, the interior of the craft was consumed by flames. Black smoke, thick and suffocating, filled the air. It spread to the cockpit, blocking all visibility for the pilots. There was no time to call for help. The chopper spiraled out of control.

Someone screamed, "BRACE FOR IMPACT!"

Nick huddled down, close to the floor, tightening his security belt. Screeching steel. Impact. *Nothingness.* The machine struck the water with the force of an asteroid. He lost consciousness. Everything became a tumbling, rolling blur of metal. The freezing Atlantic poured in, rushing through every crack.

When he came to, Nick was sinking rapidly, disappearing beneath the sea. His fingers fumbled for the safety belt. With a click, he swam through swirling chaos. When he broke the surface, he tried to swim, but his left arm screamed in agony. The water was freezing, and within minutes, he was losing dexterity. Struggling to inflate his life preserver, he clung to a piece of wreckage for warmth, heat still radiating in the metal. The tumultuous swell tossed him around like a rag doll. Then, hope: the inflatable emergency raft. Nick and one other crewman clambered aboard to safety. But it was just the two of them. He had no idea where the others were. There was nothing to do but wait for rescue. Reality sunk in. Both of them were exhibiting symptoms of hypothermia. Something was severely wrong with Nick's head. The clock was against them. Nick's strength dwindled as time dragged on.

As if sensing their desperation, salvation arrived. Coast Guard blades cut through the desolation. A man in a black wet suit rappelled toward them. He looped a harness around Nick and motioned to the crew above. Within minutes, they ascended from the raft. Away from the icy waters, away from certain death.

As the helicopter made its way to the nearest hospital, Nick motioned to the man who rescued him. "If I don't make it . . . please, tell my wife I love her. I love her so much and I'm so sorry. Will you tell her, please?"

"Just hang on," he said. "We'll be there soon and you can tell her yourself."

At this, tears fill my eyes. My gaze is locked on Nick's disfigured face, and I gently squeeze his hand.

His voice softens. "When I was in the water, I fought for you, Sarah. For us, for our future. God saved me so I can get my life straight. I'm so sorry. For everything."

I nod my head, too emotional to speak. Quiet fills the air as we look at one another. Underneath the gashes and dried blood, behind the burns and bandages, I see the man I married, the man I've been fighting for, waiting for, praying for. He's back. Back from the affair. Back from near death. It's all that matters now.

A doctor arrives later in the afternoon to share the official diagnosis and next steps. Nick has a torn rotator cuff and needs stitches for multiple lacerations, but most concerning is the damage to his head.

The doctor slowly removes the thick gauze bandages wrapped around his skull. He motions to me. "Would you like to see?"

Bracing myself, I walk behind Nick. I swallow, trying not to vomit as I look down at my husband's head.

A horrific gash above his right ear stretches down toward his neck then back up to his left ear. His scalp is completely sliced open. The skin has been violently torn apart. The white of his skull shines through ragged clumps of bloody, torn tissue. I swallow again. *Pull it together, be strong.*

"How bad is it?" Nick asks.

"It's not pretty," I say. Nick's helmet most likely saved his life, but it also nearly scalped him.

The doctor clears his throat. "Honestly, it's a miracle you survived.

As of now, we're on schedule to get you into surgery this evening. But I'll come by later to check in on you."

A barrage of text messages and calls arrive as news of the crash spreads. All afternoon we keep the television on, anxiously awaiting updates on the other crew members as information is released. We ask each doctor, nurse, and military representative, but no one seems to know. Then, we hear the broadcast.

One of the crew members is still missing; his body has not yet been recovered from the water. Another was pronounced dead on arrival. The one who had been rescued on the raft with Nick is faring well, no serious injuries. One—my Nick—is listed in critical condition. The remaining crewman, one of the pilots, is undergoing surgery. A doctor tells us it looks promising for him, there's hope. Later in the evening, we hear the news . . . He too has passed. Nick is only one of two survivors. Three men are dead.

All the light and hope are sucked out of the room. Nick's face grows dark. The news settles around him with a tangible weight.

"Turn it off," he demands sharply. I click off the television and watch him with concern.

Everything feels surreal. It was just another flight, a routine training mission, one of countless he'd been on. *How can it be?* I think of the other crew members' wives, their children. My heart aches at their unimaginable grief. Downstairs, one of the wives would lie with her husband's body long after it had grown cold—refusing to leave his side. That so easily could have been me.

The staff arrive at 9:20 p.m. to wheel Nick into surgery. I kiss him goodbye and whisper into his ear, "I'll be here. I love you more than anything."

"It'll be fine," he assures me. "I'll see you soon."

I offer a weak smile, but as soon as the door closes behind him, I slump heavily against the wall. Lori and her mom stop by to console me, but I just want a moment to be alone with my thoughts, to process the horror of everything that's transpired. Fear flits through my mind. *What if something goes wrong in surgery?* When I'm finally left in the quiet, I sit in the dark, utterly exhausted, but unable to sleep.

I wait for hours, my anxiety increasing with every passing minute. Around 3:30 a.m., they wheel Nick back in. The sight of him with fresh bandages permits a sigh of relief. The doctor tells me it took over two hundred staples and stitches to put his scalp back together—his skull resembles something out of Frankenstein—but in time, he will recover.

With my husband in my line of sight, I nestle back into the hospital chair and finally let sleep wash over me.

I don't leave the hospital room for three days. I refuse to leave Nick's side. Not to shower, not for fresh air. I barely eat. He slowly stabilizes as visitors file in and out. There are military officials asking for statements, hospital staff, friends, coworkers, even Nick's mother, who gets flown in from California.

His physical pain is unrelenting. The constant supply of medication helps, but the wounds have been incurred on his soul as much as his body. I see the mental and emotional toll—his anguish and anger, mostly the looming question of why.

He asks me, "Why did I survive when better men didn't?" As if being spared is about deservingness. Tragedy doesn't discern. He struggles to reconcile it, wrestling with a sense of guilt. His eyes are shadowed from lack of sleep, and his pale face is locked in a grimace of suffering. Even when these scars fade, the crash will live under his skin, etched into permanent places.

The doctors are concerned that fluids could build up in his brain and cause swelling, putting pressure on his sensitive scalp. To remedy this, they install a shunt—a hollow tube that runs from his brain outside the base of his skull and into a clear pouch tucked into his hospital gown. The excess fluid drains from his head into the pouch and gets emptied every few hours by the nurses. Before he's discharged, they instruct me how to clear the line and dump the contents.

I run my fingers as gently as possible along the tube, siphoning off the airflow from top to bottom, as Nick cringes in pain. When I get it clear, I unscrew the pouch and empty it into the sink. The greenish-yellow liquid smells as it swirls down the drain and I try not to gag.

His left arm is useless until he can get rotator cuff surgery, which will take months to rehabilitate. I have to be vigilant with his Frankenstein head gash, watching for infection and cleaning the flesh underneath the staples and stitches routinely. There is an overwhelming number of medications: pain medication, medication for swelling, medication to sleep, medication for regular bowel movements since the others cause constipation. Nick requires an array of pills that need to be administered at regimented hours. I take detailed notes and create a schedule.

All day, I sit next to him and hold his hand. When there is a moment of quiet, Nick and I talk about us. With our heads close together, he promises me, "This is my second chance. To be a better man, to treat you right. To not take you for granted, to love you like I should."

With every word, my heart fills with hope. I have my husband back. Here he is, saying what I most need to hear, promising to be the man I married. And just like that, all the suffering, the hopelessness, the despair, the hurt—it isn't all I see. Our love can be saved. Against all odds. With every breath he takes, clarity arrives. He survived . . . we can survive.

8

THE WIDOWS

After three long days at the hospital, Nick and I get approval to go home. While I can't wait to sleep in our bed, to take a hot shower, the responsibility weighs heavy. Nick's caretaking falls solely on my shoulders. Thankfully, my generous coworkers from the nonprofit donate their own hard-earned vacation hours so I can stay home.

Daryn and Cat had come to the hospital immediately after the crash. They hugged me tightly and offered, "Anything you need, we're here for you. Don't even think about work." The time off will be necessary. While he's no longer in critical condition, Nick still needs 24/7 care.

The first night, we try to sleep in our bed, but the back of his head is so sensitive that lying down is impossible. Unable to get comfortable, only the couch offers respite. I pull blankets and a pillow to the floor beside him so I can get him anything he needs. This section of carpet will be my bed for weeks.

Every day I dress him, gently pulling a shirt over his head, trying to avoid contact with his delicate scalp. I negotiate getting his injured arm in the sleeve, then readjust his sling as he moans. I bathe him in a shallow bath to avoid getting his head wet. I adhere to the medication schedule throughout the night, setting alarms and waking up in the dark to administer his prescriptions. The worst part is emptying the brain fluid. He groans in agony every time I siphon the liquid. A demanding reality sets in as taking care of him becomes my new normal.

At twenty-three, I never imagined I would become a full-time caregiver for my husband. That the fit man who just days ago was lifting weights in the gym now can't do anything without my help. We have no idea of our capacity to be strong until the unimaginable becomes reality and we must rise to the occasion.

The days pass in a blur—more texts and calls from California, a constant stream of people in and out of our apartment: military officials take down report after report for their investigation, Nick's family, mutual friends, our pastor, even strangers who drop off meals and donate an Xbox. When tragedy strikes, the generosity of people is revealed. These overwhelming amounts of kindness can never be repaid, but they make all the difference. Still, emotional and mental exhaustion descend with the overwhelm. Numbness sets in. I go through the necessary motions—smiling, playing host, taking care of Nick—but I slip into a state of survival. My limited capacity feels like a fragile wavering flame in the face of a tidal wave.

All the while, Nick retreats further into grief and guilt. Plagued by the haunting question of why, he suffers behind an unbreachable defense. When he sinks into this darkness, there is no pulling him into the light. I wait on the other side, hoping he will appear, even if briefly, to connect with him, to have him here. But he's adrift in his own sea of pain, and this time, there is no miraculous rescue.

Nick and I attend the first funeral and meet the pilot's wife, Sasha. She sits in front of the packed church with her young children. Long, wavy brown hair frames a grief-stricken face; her eyes are red-rimmed from crying. A closed coffin sits before us. Pew after pew of silent onlookers fill the cold cathedral. Nick and I sit with other members of his unit. Various military officials and clergy make speeches; even Nick rises to say a few words. After the formalities, Sasha walks to the coffin, the final resting place of her husband. It's tradition to adorn it with aircrewman wings.

Nick whispers a sharp command in my ear: "Don't cry." I nod solemnly.

Sasha pushes the gold wings down into the soft, glossy wood. A heart-splitting wail escapes her lips, echoing through the airy arches. I clench my body, trying not to let the tears spill out that have welled in my eyes. Then, aircrewman after aircrewman rise to push their wings into the deceased pilot's encasement. The sound is a harsh, sharp, reverberating thud as each gets slammed into the wood. Pallbearers carry the casket outside. A bugle sounds mournfully; a gun salute cracks through the sky. An American flag is gently folded and handed to Sasha, whose shaking hands accept all that is offered to her in place of her husband.

That evening, Nick and I visit her home along with a gathering of friends and family. We walk into a crowded kitchen brimming with food, conversation, and alcohol. She wants to hear details of the crash directly from Nick. They leave for a walk, and I find myself alone in the living room, sitting on an ottoman, gazing at photos of a man who no longer draws breath. They are gone for thirty minutes, then an hour. I grow increasingly uneasy as the night wears on.

I understand the need to know—I would want to know—but underneath the compassion for a woman who has just lost the love of her life and the father of her children, I can't quell the deeply embedded uneasiness about my husband. When they return from the winter night, their faces are flushed. Nick sits down beside me while Sasha settles on the couch across from us.

"Thanks for letting me steal your husband," she says, her eyes meeting mine.

I drive Nick home in a silence that stretches beyond a space neither of us can fill.

⁓

A few days later, Nick and I visit another widow, Christine. Her late husband's entire family is gathered in their small apartment. They greet us with hugs as they welcome us at the door. *What a strange thing*, I think, *to hug the survivor of the crash that claimed your own son, brother, husband . . . What questions they must have for God.*

Christine and her late husband, Ben, had just celebrated their one-year anniversary. She's in her early twenties with bleached blonde hair, her dark eyes shadowed by sleeplessness. Photos of them line the walls; they peer down at us as we squeeze onto the couch. In the frames, they are so happy, so young, so unaware of the tragedy ahead.

Nick starts at the beginning. I know this can't be easy. He speaks slowly, answering questions, recounting what transpired, giving as much detail as he can. He trails off when he arrives at the rescue, which ultimately came too late for Ben. They know the rest.

We stay gathered in the living room as they reminisce. All the while, a prevailing sadness hangs in the air. We can acknowledge the loss, but the void left is eternal. When we go to say goodbye, I hug Christine tightly, whispering how sorry I am. The apology feels meaningless. Ben's family embraces Nick in gratitude as he tells Christine, "If I can do anything, anything at all, please let me know." She smiles tearfully and hugs him goodbye.

⁓

Nick, his mother, and I are leaving a memorial for the crew members on the military base when his phone rings. He sits in the passenger seat, his mother in the back. I navigate out of the parking lot as he answers the call on speakerphone.

"Hello?"

A man's voice on the other end fills the car. "Is this Nick?"

He confirms.

"Nick, this is Mark Wahlberg."

I slam on the brakes at a stop sign and look at Nick, wide-eyed. Momentarily stunned, he mumbles, "No way . . . c'mon, man. Seriously?"

"Seriously," says Mark on the other end. "Listen, I wanted to call and tell you how sorry I am to hear about the accident. You boys do really good work for our country. Thank you for your service. You make us all proud." The Boston accent is now clearly recognizable.

I try not to squeal with excitement. Nick's face glows. "Thank you..." he stutters. "Thank you so much, *Mark*."

"Nick, how you doin'? What are you up to?"

"Honestly . . . it's been tough. We're just leaving a memorial . . . I'm with my mom and wife in the car."

"You be strong now and you'll get through," says Mark. "Listen, do you like to work out?"

Nick sighs. "One of my greatest passions. But sadly, it'll be a while before I can get back in the gym with these injuries."

"Tell you what," says Mark, "I've got a new line of workout products coming out. I'd like to send you some. I'll have my assistant call you later to get your address. How does that sound?"

"That would be really amazing," says Nick. "Thank you so much."

"Of course. Tell your wife and mother hello for me. You take care of yourself, Nick. Thank you again for your service."

It's the first time I see Nick smile in what seems like ages. A glimmer of his old spark during these dark days.

I fidget in my seat on the stage, pulling my skirt lower. Light shines in my face, making it difficult to see into the audience. Next to me sits Nick, a beanie pulled low over his scarred head. His left arm still hangs in a sling, offset by a blue button-up. His face appears calm, but I can feel his trepidation. The pastor of the church we've been attending for the past year has asked Nick if he would speak. He said Nick's story of survival is a testament to God's faith, and if Nick would be willing, he should share it as an inspiration to others. After all, God had given him a second chance.

The pastor has no idea about the struggles in our marriage. The affair is the elephant in the room of our relationship. Even now, with Nick's clear commitment, we don't talk about it. It's on the back burner, relegated for a time when he has more capacity. Yet I think of it incessantly. His infidelity didn't sink with the helicopter. My broken heart didn't get stitched up like the injury to his scalp. He promises that he no longer speaks to photo girl and substantiates the claim, offering his phone as evidence—the start of our open phone policy. For now, it has to be enough; I have to be patient and wait. His recovery is more important. While so much lies ahead, at least I'm not fighting alone anymore. I pull myself from my thoughts and glance over at Nick.

I hadn't anticipated sitting with him on stage. At the last minute the pastor asked me to join, so here I am, feeling vulnerable and on display. Nick and I both know he has to be careful with every word. The military investigation into the cause of the crash is underway, and he can't jeopardize his career by releasing any information to the public until the report is official. Nick had invited the widows and their families to attend. I can just make out Christine's face in the packed church.

The interview unfolds as the pastor takes my husband through the events of the fateful day. Nick recounts the incident: how he wasn't supposed to fly that day, how quickly the crash had happened, praying for survival, unsure if he was destined for heaven or hell.

"I begged God in the water for a second chance to be a better man, a better husband." As he says this, he glances toward me. I place my hand gently on his shoulder. "The path to destruction is broad and I was on it. I was on the fast track . . . Everything at home starts falling apart and you start falling apart. I wasn't in a good place."

The pastor wags his head and responds, "You can lose what's important to you when you're caught up in the moment."

He has no idea, I think to myself. Nick talks about his fellow aircrewmen, how they were all good men, how he'll do his best to honor them through living. I wipe away a tear as they talk about the ones they left behind, their children, their wives. But Nick doesn't tear up. He barely cracks, speaking slowly, displaying little emotion.

The pastor continues, "What now? What are your intentions now that you have this second chance? What would you tell people about this opportunity to start over?"

Nick pauses. "Get my life back, get my life straight . . . God is the reason I'm here and I know that . . . You need to assess yourself, know where you stand, be honest with yourself. Because I wasn't. I was pulling a blindfold over my eyes. Now, I get to be a better man."

I sit next to my husband as he shares the story that will define the rest of our lives. I sit next to the man I love and feel so grateful to have him back. Only afterward do I realize the pastor hadn't asked me a single question. *Did he even look my way?* It strikes me as odd. Instead, I sat perched and silent. A good woman, a supportive wife, perfectly contained. On display, but not invited into the conversation. Present, but voiceless. I was happy to be there to support Nick, but in the end, I'm left feeling used. In a world where I already feel small from the affair, I feel even smaller. Just another role I have to play. I silence my own pain for his, suppressing all that rages within. Unraveling slowly happens when we're looking the other way, dead set on holding everything together.

9
UNRAVELING

With the funerals behind us, Nick will be home for months recovering. The days stretch as our visitors lessen. Three weeks later and he still sleeps on the couch while I lie vigilantly on the floor beside him. His bloodshot eyes fade back to their attractive chocolate brown. The stitches and staples get removed, but the gashes scar cherry red. The doctor removes the tube that drains his brain fluid, pulling it out slowly with a horrendous sucking sound, like when the dentist uses the small vacuum to suck water out of a patient's mouth. Aside from the sling, Nick looks like a man on the mend. Yet within, his mental suffering intensifies.

The grief, depression, and guilt seem to generate isolation. The concrete barrier he erects feels impenetrable. It's as if a lonely ache echoes off the walls and a pressure mounts between us. Increasingly volatile, he pushes everyone away with the justification that "no one could possibly understand." I apologize on his behalf for his outbursts at friends, while our relationship wavers with each mood swing. There are so many versions of Nick I've come to know. The one who swept me off my feet. The one who came back from deployment in love with another woman. This one after the crash: wounded. He's so close, yet so far.

There are brief moments of connection, not enough to satiate, but enough to give me hope. From across the couch, he'll reach for my hand and tell me, "Sarah, if it weren't for you, I probably would have died. I wouldn't have had anything to fight for." I cross the sectional and gently let my head rest on his chest. *What a beautiful thing*, I think, *what a fragile thing, a heartbeat when it was almost no more— the warmth of him when he was almost cold.*

February arrives, as does our two-year wedding anniversary. To celebrate, I make reservations at our favorite restaurant overlooking the water. I get dressed up, hoping he notices my effort. High heels, makeup, a floral dress. I wrap my hair around a curling iron while he drinks a beer in the living room. I drive us along the coast, miffed he didn't say anything when I emerged from the bedroom transformed.

After we place our orders, I creep the affair into our conversation. As much as I try to minimize it, to wait for him to be ready, whenever that may be, it looms like a shadow over my every waking moment.

"So . . . have you heard from her?" I ask, trying to sound casual.

He rolls his eyes. "Nope."

"I think we should try to go to the marriage counselor again. I know you have a lot going on, but—"

He pushes back from the table forcefully, his voice raised as he directs his anger toward me. "Seriously, Sarah . . . again? You are my biggest stressor! I can't even focus on myself because of everything going on with us."

"I don't understand," I retort. "You don't even try! There's never a right time for you to talk about us."

"What is there to discuss? It's over. I told you. I'm not talking to her anymore. I've apologized a million times. When are you going to let it go?"

"It's not that simple, Nick. You don't understand how badly this hurt. What you did..."

He snaps back, "Right, of course. I forgot. You're always right. I'm always wrong."

"That's not true."

"I can never win. I never do the right thing. I'm never good enough."

Tears pools in my eyes and run down my face. I wipe them away hurriedly.

"There you go again. Always crying. I swear that's all you do. You know, you shouldn't be the emotional one. *I* should be. I'm the one who almost died. The one who lost brothers out there."

"Then why aren't you? You never show any emotion unless it's anger."

He shrugs and looks away. Unable to contain myself any longer, I rush to the bathroom, hot tears dripping down blush-streaked cheeks. A self-conscious voice tells me that everyone in the restaurant is watching, judging. When I'm composed enough to go back to the table, I've lost my appetite. I poke a fork at cold food, the rest of dinner is strained.

At home, I lie on my makeshift bed on the floor while he plays video games on the new Xbox—a habit developed over the past weeks of recovery. But when I close my eyes, all I see is a vision of me running through the restaurant, dress flowing, eyes downcast to hide the tears, wanting to feel beautiful and desired on a day that once meant so much to us, only to feel like a pretending little fool.

One month has passed since the crash. Nick and I don't speak about it, but I can tell he's depressed. Clumps of greasy hair fall out when I clean his head. The Frankenstein staples have been replaced with an angry red welt that stretches from one side of his skull to the other. The scent of body odor fills the apartment. Since he can't shower, I wash him with a sponge in a shallow bath, but he can't lift his injured arm enough to properly clean his armpit. We get in a screaming match about his pain medication. I only give them to him at the proper intervals and in the amounts the doctor prescribed, but he demands more or takes them himself. I count his Percocet consumption—ten in a twelve-hour stretch, double his prescription. Luckily, the hospital wasn't as generous with the OxyContin. If I say anything he reacts so defensively, it escalates into another fight and only makes things worse. I watch with growing concern, especially when he drinks. Beer with dinner. Beer with the video games. Beer with more pills.

On top of his unpredictable moods, he drifts away emotionally. He texts with the widows—Christine and Sasha—almost every day. He goes to Sasha's to hang out and Christine drops by unannounced. His guilt drives him to support them however he can. I'm ashamed to admit it, but a wave of jealousy sweeps over me. I know their husbands just died and I should be more understanding, more secure. But in weak moments, the threat washes me away. He's barely speaking to me, yet his friendship with them is seemingly blossoming. My trust in him is still as fragile as eggshells, threatening to crack with each text and outing. I thought that after the funerals we would move on, focus on us, *repair*. In spite of the creeping discomfort, I convince myself the problem is me—my insecurity, my jealously. *Pick your battles, Sarah.*

I'm sleeping next to the couch when Nick's phone goes off at 1:00 a.m. My first thought from the muddled confusion of sleep is that it's photo girl.

"Who is it?" I ask in a daze.

"It's Sasha," he responds.

Why is Sasha calling in the middle of the night? He answers and talks for a few minutes in a hushed tone. I can't make out what she's saying, but he ends the call with a vague response. "I'm sorry, I can't right now . . . My wife . . . Let's talk tomorrow."

"What was that about?" I ask.

"She wants me to come over."

"For what? It's one in the morning."

"She wants me to hold her."

I'm jolted wide awake. "Are you serious?"

He's quiet, choosing his words carefully. "She said it helps her sleep, having people there for her. Otherwise, she gets nightmares and it's hard to be alone."

Do I really have to explain to him that this isn't normal? That her calling and asking this of him, a married man, is completely inappropriate? Do I really need to enforce this kind of boundary? The worst part is that in the silence between us, I can tell he wants to go. He wants to be there for her. As I lie on the carpet, on the living room floor where I've slept for weeks, my anger swirls.

"No," I say flatly. "You're not going."

"I know," he says quietly.

But in between us is a world of unspoken resentment, wedging itself even deeper as we let the silence stretch. I understand that grief makes people do strange things, but at this, I draw the line.

The next morning, I raise my concerns in the light of day.

"None of this is normal," I start. "It's like the affair—"

"It's a completely different situation!" he snaps, his voice rising. "Her husband just died. She's grieving! She said people come stay with her every night, even her neighbors. You're being so selfish, Sarah! You only think about yourself."

I'm temporarily lost for words. *Is he right? Am I the problem?* If I was the one who lost a husband, would I be calling his colleague to come over at 1:00 a.m. for comfort? My head spun. The whole thing feels so insane it actually makes me wonder if I'm crazy.

"Nick... I know she's grieving. I understand you want to support her, but this is totally inappropriate. Do you not see that?"

He erupts, "It's always my fault, isn't it! You know what it is? I'm just not good enough for you. I swear, I'm like a cancer to you. I make you sick. You'd be better off without me."

I recoil. "That's not true. I care about us, Nick. I love you—"

"Well, you shouldn't," he says. "Honestly, I should've just died in the crash. It would've been better that way."

"Don't say that, Nick. Please. Never say that."

Silent, he looks out the living room window as a shadow crosses his face. That's it. Our fights reach this place where he draws an absolute and I'm unable to reach him. There's no convincing him otherwise, no room for further conversation. He pulls out his phone, signaling he's done.

He slips away all over again, only this time he's not on the other side of the world, he's right beside me. I feel helpless to change his trajectory. The widows, their needs, Nick's guilt that will drive him to cross all boundaries. It's too much. After the crash, he was so committed and genuine. *What happened?*

Over the following days, he casually makes comments that turn my blood cold. "You know, I check out other women when we're together, wondering if I can get with them... There are things I hate about you... Sometimes I think the only reason I'm with you is because I never had you in high school."

The proclamations sting, fueling pitiful feelings, reminiscent of an all-too-familiar situation where I am resigned to suffer under the belief I can save us, that I can win my husband back from wherever it is he's headed. It's astounding what we can be blind to about ourselves when we're so focused on someone else.

Recent words from a friend sound in my head, warning me, "You need to do your own thing, Sarah. You're way too accessible to Nick, so you end up being his scapegoat. He takes everything out on you. You need to give him space. He has to find his way without making you at fault for everything." I know they're right. I also know I'm too terrified to give him space—I don't trust what he would do with it.

I carry the weight of it all, but the burden is becoming unbearable. It shows in the dark circles underneath my eyes, the constant stress keeping my stomach in knots, the thoughts that fill my mind: a helicopter falling from the sky, Nick in bed with photo girl, Sasha looking at me with gleaming eyes as she says, "Thanks for letting me steal your husband."

What my friend didn't say in the face of my fragility is an even harder truth: What I'm tolerating from Nick speaks volumes about *me*.

10

WAKING UP

I sneak into the back row of the packed yoga studio, strategically placing myself as out of sight as possible. I've never been to a yoga class before; the fit and confident people in front of me clearly have. Some gaze at themselves stretching in the mirror; others lie on their backs, extended on their mats. A woman in spandex shorts pops up into an effortless handstand. I avoid my reflection and self-consciously look away from show-off spandex lady.

In college, a friend told me that hot yoga was an amazing workout. "You sweat buckets," she said, "then you feel so amazing afterward. Sometimes people fart . . . but you would totally love it."

I never joined her for the sweaty-fart experience. But when I saw a Groupon for a studio up the street, I figured the workout couldn't hurt. Maybe I can get Nick's words out of my head. Sitting on the mat, I shake myself from my thoughts. *I'm just here to sweat. Easy enough, it feels like a sauna. It must be over one hundred degrees.*

The instructor walks in, a toned, young brunette who introduces herself as Lise. Lise seats herself in the front of the room. After a welcome, she ominously says, "If you get overheated just lie down and rest, but please do your best not to leave the room. The temperature swings won't be good for you unless you have time to properly cool down."

I conceal my apprehension as spandex lady sits in full lotus pose, smiling like a psychopath. Her confidence is irksome, mostly because I have none left myself. Lise presses play on the stereo and promptly tells us what to do. She says a name and I gather it's a posture as the people in front of me begin to move their bodies. Thankfully, she follows with cues about what to adjust. Soon, I lose myself in her commands. I do my best to fumble along, mimicking the strangers in front of me. Sweat drips down my forehead and trickles along the back of my neck. Before I know it, I'm soaking wet, huffing for air.

As I try to perch with one foot on the floor and the other foot pressed into my upper inner thigh—"like a tree"—I lose my balance. It catches Lise's attention, and she gently invites me to "Get back in." *I'm trying!* I scream in my head at her annoying sweat-free face. I gasp for breath, counting the minutes, desperate for cool air and sweet reprieve. For what feels like an eternity, we stretch and move in the heat, putting our bodies in an assortment of positions. Finally, to my great relief, Lise tells us to lie down. *Thank God.*

My legs relax as my arms rest on the hardwood floor, palms face up. Sweat drips onto the already drenched towel underneath me. Savasana, the final pose. Lise's feet pad softly across the room as she turns off the lights. Music plays quietly in the background. The dark feels safe, like a cocoon. Lyrics float across the studio and I strain to catch the words. Something about being brave after a storm, a sister in need who is not alone.

Lise's voice is quiet and soft when she says, "Remember, everything is temporary, nothing is permanent."

Maybe it's the eerily resonant music. Or Lise's words. Maybe it's the safety of darkness. Or the exhaustion of carrying so much for so long. But a chord is struck. My fists are clenched, eyes squeezed tight, chest shaking from holding in sobs that desperately want to surface. I can no longer pretend that I'm in control or that I have what it takes or that I'm not absolutely miserable. I can no longer hold back the emotion—the crying that feels forbidden at home. I come undone.

Hot tears burn my cheeks as they slide down the sides of my face. I cry hard, silently, my body shaking on the rubber mat. Sweat and tears pool underneath me. I let it all go. The studio feels like a church, a sacred place, like discovering holy in the depths of hell.

Lise says it again. "Everything is temporary, nothing is permanent." I swear these words are meant for me. I grasp at them, my final, fragile hope. Something in my heart shifts. *Everything is temporary.* It has to be. This can't last forever. *God,* I beg, *help me get through this. Please . . . give me strength.*

When Lise says, "Namaste," I'm startled out of my emotional Savasana. I self-consciously roll up my mat and wipe my beet-red, swollen face with a towel. I can't explain what just occurred, but it feels like the only right thing in a sea of wrongness.

Over the following weeks, hot yoga becomes my haven, the place I run to when everything feels unbearable. It's the only place I can get out of my head as I struggle through the postures. The workout does something to me, unlocks something in me. I set up in the back row, barefoot on a rented mat, avoiding eye contact. Every time I take a class, I feel a little bit more confident—not annoying spandex-lady confident, but still. I slowly reclaim a sense of strength and self-esteem that had been obliterated. For whatever reason, sweating like a pig while fumbling with squeezed butt cheeks gives me the fortitude to make it through another day. Desperation breeds receptiveness.

Anything that feels like hope, like pulling the shattered pieces back together, whatever that thing is, can become a lifeline. Yoga becomes mine.

~

Nick and I go out to an early dinner to celebrate Valentine's Day. We sit across from each other in a booth, but his attention lingers on a television at the bar. We have little to say and silence fills most of the evening. We got in a fight before even leaving the apartment. He'd gifted me a necklace, but I didn't want to wear it since it didn't match my outfit. I try to make small talk, stirring the straw of my passion fruit mojito, but when I glance back at him, his eyes are on his phone, his fingers tapping a text, mind elsewhere.

All of a sudden, I imagine looking at us objectively, as if I were a stranger passing by. I would note the lack of intimacy, the nonexistent connection. I notice with detachment how hard I'm trying, but underneath the trying is something else: boredom. I'm struck by the thought. It has never once crossed my mind. The man across from me is neither interesting nor engaging; there is no scintillating conversation, no effort, no vulnerability.

Even the necklace he'd given me feels like a gesture void of genuine consideration. For fear of being a petulant, spoiled brat (which I undoubtedly can be), I accepted the gift gratefully. How dare I complain about a gift? But the thing is, it doesn't feel like a gift. It's the broom we'll use to brush more shit under the rug. It's a necklace I never would have picked out for myself. The gifts he'd given me were usually the same ones he would (and had) given his mom. Just like the "Forever Rose." *The world's longest-lasting luxury rose, a real blossom preserved in twenty-four-karat gold!* What does one do with a handmade, timeless, one-of-a-kind Forever Rose? I hid it in a drawer, where it wouldn't ever wilt or fade. *How well does he even know me?* The only reason I'll wear the necklace will be solely for him and wanting to placate him—to avoid another fight, I'll do it.

Sitting across from Nick, it hits me. As the dust from the rubble of our marriage is settling, it isn't the heartbreak or depression, loneliness or rejection that I feel. At least, not in this moment. It's boredom. It's playing a version of his mom. It's feeling *unknown* in my most personal relationship. I could have laughed into my cocktail at the bizarreness of these thoughts. I've been so busy fighting for him and trying to save our marriage I hadn't stopped and asked myself: *Am I really willing to do this for the rest of my life?* I sit with the question through dinner. It keeps me more company than he does.

I meet friends at a church service, Cal and his wife Maggie—a couple who have become a source of support since the crash—along with Max and Trina. Max and Trina live in the same housing complex and work in the same branch of the military as Nick. Max and Trina live nearby and are also in the military. They've been our closest friends since before deployment. We've shared game nights and dinners, even served as witnesses at their wedding. In the days following the crash they were my lifeline, bringing clothes and coffee to the hospital. They're some of the only friends I've confided in about the affair and the growing struggle between Nick and me. It was Max, his short blond hair, eyes filled with concern, who told me I needed to do my own thing, to give Nick space. Trina, with her golden skin and easy laugh, who has become my companion for hot yoga classes and gym workouts. After the service, I invite Max and Trina back to the apartment for lunch. As we walk up the stairs to the second-story apartment, Trina asks where Nick is.

I pause. "Honestly . . . I'm not sure. He has a friend visiting from California, so I think they're out somewhere . . ." I trail off. Since his friend's arrival they've been out drinking almost every night and disappearing during the day. The nearby strip club crosses my mind as a possibility.

Although Nick is on medical leave—a time intended for home recovery after the injuries sustained in the crash—he's out partying and drinking as often as he can. When I'd confronted him about it, he'd laughed and said, "I was just in a helicopter crash. You really think they'll reprimand me?" Unfortunately, he's probably right.

I turn the key in the lock, swinging the door open. Something is wrong. The shades are drawn. Lights off. The living room smells of body odor and stale air.

I look over to see Nick's head bent down toward the granite countertop of the kitchen island. An open bottle. Crushed pills. A white line. The bill he's using to snort. His friend laughing by his side.

Max and Trina walk in behind me and freeze.

Anger makes my voice shake, but incredulousness keeps it low . . . pointed and sharp as a knife. "Are you serious?"

"What?" he says haughtily, grinning. "I'm not doing anything."

I want to slap the stupid smirk off his face. My eyes flash. I look back at Max and Trina. "I'm so sorry . . . you should probably go." They retreat through the open door, and I close it quickly behind them.

I turn and explode. "Are you kidding me? What the fuck do you think you're doing?" Silence. I shake my head in disgust. "This is so pathetic." He looks past me as if I'm invisible and only getting smaller by the second. His friend is motionless by his side. I continue, "I can't help you if you refuse to help yourself!" Still, he says nothing.

Seething, I stare at him. *Enough*. I'm so embarrassed by him, so resentful. From relegating the affair to playing caregiver, I've had it. All the times I metered out his pills, slept on the floor, woke up in the middle of the night, drained his brain fluid, bathed him, clothed him, fed him, cleaned up after him, sat at doctor's appointments, drove him, all to be treated like I don't matter, like our relationship doesn't matter. His blank face stares past me and reflects all that I can expect: *nothing*.

I stride into the bedroom and throw clothes into a duffel bag. Their voices murmur in the kitchen and Nick's hollow laughter sounds. Walking out, bag over my shoulder, I glance at him.

"I'm leaving. I can't do this anymore. Let me know when you decide to wake the fuck up."

The closing of the door and the crossing of the threshold mark the first steps I take as a woman who, herself, is finally waking the fuck up.

11

DARKNESS

Nick decides to stay with a friend temporarily, so a few days later, I move back into our apartment alone. Max and Trina help me call the doctor at his unit to let them know what had transpired. Even without the threat of abusing his meds, I grow increasingly worried about his mental health. Does he mean it when he says things would be better if he was gone, if he'd just died? It isn't the first time he's made suicidal comments, and it keeps me in a constant state of concern for his well-being.

Nick had a friend and fellow aircrewman die by suicide less than a year ago. No one saw it coming. Eli had been struggling with severe depression and shot himself in the head. One bullet didn't do the trick. Barely conscious, in a pool of his own blood, he pulled the trigger again. That's why, Nick tells me offhandedly, if he's going to kill himself, it'll be with a heavier caliber handgun.

Even without him home, Nick stalks the edges of my sanity.

It's almost nine o'clock one evening when a restlessness sets in. I can't shake the feeling that something is wrong. It starts quietly, a nagging sensation in my gut. I try to stifle the rising discontent, but it spreads into every cell. Nick is everywhere. I'm surrounded by us. Our photos. Our memories. I'm haunted by the man I love, even if he's become a stranger. I can't shake that as his wife, I still feel responsible. I thought leaving would be a temporary measure, that space might bring him back. My mind is not yet ready to acknowledge the possibility that this could be permanent.

I pick up my phone to text him. Immediately, I set it back down. *Don't*, I tell myself. But denial is my Achilles' heel. Waking up to the truth can be a slow and painful process. It doesn't happen all at once. Backsliding is a shockingly swift and slippery slope. One day I will have to reconcile what it is in me that believes I need someone like him—that thinks this is love—I will have to account for my own behavior. But today is not that day.

I pick up my phone again. Begging more than hoping, my fingers tap a text. *Will he come?* All I want in this moment is him. Even as I hate myself for it. He texts back:

It's pouring outside. I don't want to drive in the rain.

The disparity is blatant. It hits me like a freight train. I still would have gone to the ends of the earth for him. The panic spreads, like ants teeming all over me. I want to crawl out of my skin, out of my very life.

Under the cover of dark, I walk to my car. The winter night howls, a bitter wind greeting me. I drive to the beach. When I park, I look down to realize I hadn't even bothered to change my clothes. Pajama shorts and a thin black sweatshirt are no defense against the chill. In a haze, I hadn't grabbed shoes. I lock my car and walk barefoot to the beach. As soon as I reach the sand, the wind whips it up with such force it bites my legs with sharp stings. The waves, small and angry, pummel the shoreline. White foam silhouetted in the darkness.

The anger of the storm becomes my own. All that I have buried for so long, willed away, becomes an unstoppable tempest. My body grows hot. I'm angry. Beyond angry. I'm furious with Nick. For breaking his promises and breaking my heart. For closing himself off and becoming so righteous. I'm enraged with the military. With photo girl. With the widows. I'm angry at just about everything and everyone, but mostly I'm angry with myself.

I'm the one who forgave, who stayed, who fought, who gave so much of myself to make *us* work. *I'm* the foolish one. How many nights had I cried myself to sleep? How many panic attacks had consumed me? *Why*, I'd wondered, *does love hurt so much? Why is it so hard?* In the beginning, obsession felt like love. Control felt like safety. Fights felt like passion. Jealousy a twisted compliment. For so long, I'd made excuse after excuse for every red flag only to arrive all alone to this awful, forsaken place.

My body can barely contain this bitter realization. I start to run in the cement-like sand. My feet struggle against the wet grains. I race along the shoreline as hard, fast, and far as I can. The frigid air bites at my lungs; the wind tears through my hair as a freezing rain pelts my face. The downpour soaks my sweatshirt and shorts. I sprint until I can't anymore. I can't outrun myself, can't outrun my life.

Gasping, I stop and let the ocean submerge my feet. I gaze out into the dark expanse of the Atlantic Ocean and imagine the helicopter crash just miles away. I hate who Nick has become. Who I've become.

"Fuck you," I whisper. Quietly, like a mantra. I can't stop myself. "Fuck you, fuck you, fuck you." Each time brings more anger, less restraint. I grow louder. "FUCK YOU! FUCK YOU! FUCK YOU!" I'm screaming as loud as I can. I yell to no one but the rain and wind and cold. I rage at the uncaring ocean until I lose my voice, until I lose my very spirit.

I look out at the tumultuous sea. I'd come to this beach in desperation, and I realize that I'm running not just from the hopelessness of what my marriage has become but from the woman who is so acquainted with denial that it's become her reality. It's too much, too overwhelming, a darkness I can no longer outpace.

I hang my head and walk back to the car in silence, soaking wet. I drive home and crawl into an empty bed. This dark is inescapable; there is no more light, no more fight. It presses down on me, terrifying in its intensity. It wraps its heavy cloak around me and whispers, *You are mine.*

12

TERROR

I sleep at Max and Trina's most nights. I can't stay at the apartment. Being alone feels daunting, dangerous. The darkness preys on my isolation. For now, it's safer to numb myself with the company of others.

We sit together in their living room watching television. But I'm distracted. I refresh social media, obsessively checking Nick's posts. It's Saturday night and he's out partying, celebrating Saint Patrick's Day. With each drunken photo, I debate whether or not I should intervene. It's been almost two weeks since the drug-snorting incident. He was reported to his chain of command, who I'd hoped were monitoring him, but Nick seems just as reckless. We text back and forth as his messages reflect a growing inebriation. I waver. Rescue him or leave it be? As the night grows late, I give in to the absurdity that maybe I can help. Like an addict convincing herself this time things will be different, I grab my keys and tell Max and Trina that I'll see them later.

It's 10:40 p.m. when I pull up outside the bar. As I walk in, he's impossible to miss. Adorned in St. Paddy's garb, green paint is smeared across his cheeks, beer spilled down his chest. He teeters next to the bar, empty glass in hand. His surprise to see me is evident in his far-off gaze.

"We're leaving," I inform him. "I'm taking you home."

He looks at his friends and shrugs his shoulders, to my surprise not picking a fight. As we walk toward the car, he stumbles, slurring his speech. The apartment isn't far, fifteen minutes north, but I wonder if driving a little longer might help him sober up. I continue driving straight where I should've turned for home. Through a drunken haze, he notices.

"Where are you taking me?!"

"Home, Nick. I'm just taking you home."

"What, to a fucking intervention?!"

I roll my eyes. "No, Nick, not to an intervention. It's just us going home."

"I DON'T BELIEVE YOU, BITCH! I'M NOT GOING." He unbuckles his seat belt and starts to open the passenger door.

"NICK!" I scream. I'm driving forty miles per hour. I reach over the narrow expanse of car to grab him, the door barely shutting.

"DON'T FUCKING TOUCH ME!" he roars, slapping my hand away and pushing me forcefully back to the driver's side.

His aggression shakes me. Trembling behind the wheel, I stay quiet as I navigate back home and turn into the apartment complex.

As soon as we get inside and I close the door behind us, the fight escalates. The room feels suffocating, hot, dangerous. I stand in the kitchen, on the other side of the island, a safe buffer between us. With tense shoulders, he paces back and forth in the living room.

"Why did you even pick me up? You don't give a shit about me. You left me, remember?"

"You're different, Nick," I snap back. "You've changed, and everyone sees it but you. Even your own friends—"

"What?! My friends? I see. So, you're talking about me behind my back. Why am I not surprised?"

"You push everyone away by feeling sorry for yourself. You act like such an asshole. You've become so selfish and you don't even see it."

His face becomes crimson with anger; his eyes flash as he quickens his pace across the carpet. Immediately, I doubt my outburst. I shouldn't have said anything. I know better—he's too drunk. He stalks to the wall where our wedding photos hang and rips one off, throwing it violently to the ground.

"It doesn't matter anymore, does it? None of it matters."

One by one he rips photos from the wall, throwing them across the room, continuing his tirade. "You don't care. You could never understand." He pauses, his body wavering. "No one does. I might as well be dead."

With that, he strides to the bedroom and locks the door behind him. I lean heavily into the island, trying to catch my breath. He's made these comments before. But with a flash of horror, it hits me . . . *The guns!* All of the guns are still stored under the bed. *What if he isn't being dramatic? What if he means it?* I rush to the door and jiggle the handle.

"Nick?" I say. Then I hear it, the unlocking of a gun case. *NO. NO. NO.*

"NICK!" I scream, begging, "Let me in. Unlock the door." I bang on the wood, pounding my fists against the barrier. "Please, Nick. Let me in. Don't do this."

I throw the weight of my body against the door, but it doesn't budge. "Please, Nick!"

I hear his muffled voice from the other side. "It doesn't matter. You don't care. Nothing matters anymore."

Terrified, I scream hysterically and bang harder. *It can't happen like this. It can't.*

"Please, Nick. Just let me in, unlock the door."

My mind races. Any second now I could hear the unimaginable. I look at the door and size it up. *I can kick it in, just like in the movies.* I step back and gather my strength. Swinging up, I kick my right leg as hard as I can. It doesn't budge. *Shit.* Frantic, I run back to the kitchen and open the tool drawer. I grab the first thing I see, a hammer. I bound back to the door. "Nick, please . . . please, don't do this. You don't have to do this."

"Shut the fuck up!" he yells. "I don't want to hear you crying."

With that, I bring the hammer down on the doorknob. WHACK. The sound cracks through the apartment.

"What are you doing, you psycho bitch?"

I bring it down again. WHACK. Harder. WHACK. The knob jangles precariously. One last WHACK and it breaks off completely. I push in the door.

Nick stands on the other side of the room. He's holding a handgun against his head. My heart stops.

"Nick . . . please lower the gun," I plead, walking slowly toward him. I stand in front of him, inches of space between us. Anger radiates across his face, his eyes swimming in its fire. Underneath the cover of alcohol, all I see is pain. Endless amounts of pain. "Please," I say softly, "don't do this."

We stand silent for what feels like an eternity, the pistol hovering against his temple. Only the sound of ragged breathing fills the room, torment etched on both of our faces. Slowly, after what feels like a lifetime, he lowers the gun.

As if nothing has transpired, he tosses it casually onto the bed. He walks out of the bedroom and glances at the dangling door handle.

"I'm not paying for that," he says flatly.

Adrenaline pulses through my quaking body. Tears fall uncontrollably. I'm not scared . . . *I'm terrified*. I'm terrified of him. Of what just happened. Of what he could do. I replay looking into his eyes as he held the gun to his head. There was a flash, the briefest of thoughts . . . *What if he turns the gun on me?*

With each shaky inhale, my body stops trembling and the tears slow. Silence fills the apartment. *Has he fallen asleep?* I find the courage to walk out and check on him. His body is sprawled on the couch, shoes still on, St. Paddy's garb hanging haphazardly. I watch him sleep, snoring loudly, his phone lying next to his outstretched hand. Revulsion and relief simultaneously break over me. A voice in my brain tells me to cover him with a blanket, but I don't want to touch him, don't want to be anywhere near him. I overcome my apprehension and grab the throw from the couch, spreading it across his outstretched body.

His phone vibrates with an incoming text. It's 12:30 a.m. when I glance at the home screen. Christine's name appears. *Christine? Why is one of the widows texting him so late?* The status of our open phone policy is debatable. Regardless, I reach for it and punch in the password. I slide open the message:

I miss you so much. This bed is so empty without you.

My mind goes blank.

It can't be.

Everything stops: my breath, my heart, time itself, as I stare at the message. A horrible, sick feeling sinks in. I stare at the screen, trying to find reason, but my brain has turned to mush.

I retreat with the phone to our bedroom. My hands shake all over again as I pull the now useless door closed behind me. I slide my finger across the screen and tap on their text exchanges. I start at the beginning. I read every single one.

I get halfway through when a visceral stab of rage shoots through my body like a lightning bolt. Christine had asked if he was sure about their escalating romance:

What about your wife?

He'd responded: **Don't worry, it's over between us.**

This was weeks ago. It meant that I had been holding out hope when he was already holding someone else. It meant that before I had even packed a bag, he was seducing her. It meant that they had done it right in front of me, right next to me, right under my nose. The lies he must have told her, just as he withheld the truth from me.

I had held Christine in my arms and offered her my support. I had welcomed her into my home for game nights and hangouts. I recall the last time she came over with her friend. The way she coyly looked at Nick. I served up snacks while they laughed at the table. Nick bought her flowers for her graduation. She stopped by unannounced and was surprised when I opened the door. She may have asked him about me to ease her conscience, but my heart tells me she knew better. I had dismissed all the warnings, even my own intuition that said their friendship was hiding something more as they texted every day. *How could she? Her husband was still fresh in the ground and here she was, sleeping with mine. How could he? Again . . .* The audacity, the wrongness of it all pushes me over a ledge.

I march out to the living room and stand over Nick's sleeping form. Gazing down at him, I know exactly what I want to do, something I've never done in my entire life.

I raise my right hand.

WHAP.

I slap him hard across the face.

He barely stirs from his drunken slumber.

"Is it true?" I scream, "Tell me, are you really fucking Christine?!"

He mumbles unconsciously, turning his head away. But I don't need his verbal confirmation. It's all here in front of me, even photos. The fury is unbearable; it eats into my heart and makes me blind. *This is it.* I feel crazy, unhinged, like I'm on fire and I want everything to burn.

I stride into the bedroom and climb onto our bed. I screenshot every text, every photo. It takes me over an hour to capture the escalation of their affair. I send all the proof to my phone. Collateral.

I pause. She needs to know that I know. This woman to whom I'd extended kindness and concern and hospitality. My fingers hover over the keyboard.

Hi Christine, this is Sarah, I'm sure you remember – Nick's wife. I know everything. This is so fucked-up.

It's all my brain can come up with. I hit send. A knock at the door startles me.

"Sarah, give me my phone." Nick's hand reaches through the door. Wordlessly, I rise and drop it in his outstretched palm then he retreats to the living room. It doesn't matter. I have what I need.

I lie awake for hours. There will be no sleep. I need to talk to someone. The crazy I feel threatens to unravel me completely. At 3:00 a.m., I call my best friend back in California. Thankfully, she answers, and I tell her everything. She doesn't even know about the first affair. I had kept it a secret to protect Nick. I'd confided in hardly anyone about what was really happening behind closed doors. When I reach the point where he held the gun to his head, she panics.

"Sarah, call the police! He's dangerous. You shouldn't be anywhere near him."

I consider. I recall looking into his eyes, begging him to lower the gun, how unrecognizable he was. At the time, my only concern was making sure he didn't pull the trigger. The person in front of me was unpredictable, hurting, wild. There was just anger, even hatred for me. I understand now. I shudder. I can't think about it anymore. It's over.

"No," I tell her flatly, "but I'm done. I'm so, so done."

I'm still awake at 5:00 a.m. when I get up and cross the hallway to the bathroom. I realize with horror that somehow the broken bedroom door locks itself behind me. I make my way out to the living room and sit on the sectional, as far from Nick as possible. He's tapping away on his phone; I assume doing damage control. We sit in silence as faint traces of daylight reach the window. My mind reels in shock, replaying every second, every word, every text. Piecing together timelines, questioning every interaction. *How could I have been so stupid?* The rage has seeped into every pore and sealed itself into my bones. The sight of him makes me sick. I shift my gaze to a corner of the wall, unable to look at him, trying to find words. Finally, I speak.

"I'm done, Nick. With you. With our marriage. We're over."

He sits unflinching and unreadable.

"You disgust me. That you did this to me *again* . . . That you've put me through this, not once, but over and over again. After everything I've done for you, after everything we've been through . . . and with her? Of all people, Nick. What is wrong with you? When you talked about honoring your fellow aircrewmen, is this what you had in mind?"

My tirade is met with silence, but the release is liberating. My voice rises.

"You broke us. You understand that, right? How selfish you've been . . . Clearly you don't care about the damage you cause."

He still doesn't say a word. He is completely unmoved. The lack of reaction fuels my anger.

"You're a coward, Nick. A pathetic coward." I reach the crescendo, passing the point of no return. "Honestly . . . I wish you would have just died in the crash."

The words fall out of my mouth. They hang between us on the couch, the statement unretractable. He's uttered them before, but I'd never dreamt of speaking them. Silence fills the room. He doesn't say sorry. He doesn't explain. He doesn't even blame me. There is no emotion, no regret, nothing.

Finally, he breaks the strained quiet. "I wish I did too."

I slump down, defeated. *What was the point? What was I hoping to achieve?* I don't feel any better after saying all the horrible things I just did. Just like hitting him last night, I thought it would make me feel better, but it was wholly unsatisfying.

He silently crosses the expanse of space between us on the couch. I still have tears of anger in my eyes when he tilts my head toward his. He plants his lips on mine with a kiss.

What? I pull back and shake my head, but he advances. *What's happening? I just finished telling him we're done. That I can't stand him, that he makes me sick. This doesn't make any sense.* My mind tries to string together pieces that don't fit. He leans his body against mine. I find my voice through the confusion.

"No, Nick, I don't want to."

My throat is hoarse from screaming earlier, but I say it again. He continues to ignore me and kisses me harder. Tears slide down my cheeks. My brain can't compute. *This can't be happening right now. Not after everything I just said. Not after everything he's done.*

My body freezes in disbelief at what is unfolding. Everything slows down as sharp details come into focus. My yellow-and-turquoise pajama pants. The sunlight filtering through the window. The quiet of our apartment. His pungent alcohol-laden breath on my neck.

I try to shove him away, my hands pushing up against his chest, but I'm no match for his strength. I cry harder as he slides me underneath him, pinning me in place. Still, he doesn't say a word. Somewhere a voice in my brain: *This can't be happening. This doesn't make any sense.* His weight feels suffocating, immovable. *Why am I so weak?*

"I don't want this," I say again through tears, as if it makes a difference.

I hear the words from a distance, my voice something separate. He's ripping off his gym shorts. He's peeling my underwear down my thighs. My eyes focus then freeze on a section of wall above his right shoulder. *This shouldn't be happening.*

I'm crying when he inserts himself inside of me. I'm crying as he heaves his body against mine. I'm crying as he moans into my ear. But I have no fight, no strength, nothing. Just hot tears as I whisper a final time, "I don't want this."

13

ENDINGS

Several months later, when I'll confide in a friend about all that transpired, I'll tell her, "That was the last time I had sex with my husband." But the words won't feel right. Sandpaper on my tongue, a tangled mess in my brain. It wasn't me *having* anything. What happened didn't *feel* like sex. She'll look at me with sad eyes and speak the words I hadn't yet found.

"Sarah . . . you were raped. What happened to you was marital rape."

Her declaration will shock me. It never occurred to me that one could be married *and* raped by their partner. It will be my first time hearing the term, and it will sound like too strong of an accusation. In my ignorance, my mind will race to deny it . . . *Nick loved me. He was my husband. We had sex all the time.* When I think of rape, I think of a stranger following me to my car or slipping something into my cocktail. I don't imagine the face of my husband.

Still, something in my heart will ache. An unsettled piece of the puzzle, a nagging that will refuse to be silenced. It will take several more years to be able to reconcile what occured that morning, to name the violation incurred to my body and mind.

I watch Nick retreat down the steps when he leaves later that morning, his body lumbering on the creaky floor. My stomach in knots, I know what transpired felt deeply and dreadfully wrong. But I'm too numb, too shattered, to do anything with it. I close the door behind him, bolting it quickly. Instead, his affair with Christine takes center stage. What happened was just another wound in a series of many.

I ask Max and Trina, along with Cal and Maggie—our church friends—to come over. When they arrive, we all sit at the dining room table. A pale sun shines through the window. Shaky, tearless, still in shock, I wring my hands as I recount the events of the night before. Nick trying to jump out of the car. Breaking down the door. The gun. The discovery of the affair.

"That's it," says Max. "For your safety and for his, we need to report him to the unit. He's not going to like it, but it's the right thing to do, Sarah. He needs serious help."

I chew my bottom lip. I know he's right, but Nick will be livid. He'll see this as a betrayal of trust. What choice do I have?

"Okay," I say quietly. "What about the guns?"

Max looks at Cal, who volunteers, "I can take them. We have a gun safe in our garage. Until Nick gets help and stabilizes, we'll hold onto them."

The air is tense. The responsibility of trying to save a man's life weighs heavy on all of us.

Nick's unit places him on suicide watch, which means someone will be assigned to regularly check in on him. With Max and Cal's help, we remove all the guns from the apartment.

When we talk on the phone, Nick is furious. He lambasts me, "If anything happens, it's on you. This is your fault."

"I'm worried about you, Nick . . . I'm sorry, but—"

"I can't trust anyone, can I? You betrayed my confidence. If you don't return the guns, I'll call the cops for stolen property."

"Technically, I'm still your wife, so good luck with that. I think we both know this was necessary for your safety."

"Fuck you," he says, ending the call.

I try to piece the fragments of my shattered life back together. I can only manage one thing at a time, one day at a time. I don't go back to the apartment. It's as if something has died and now haunts the space—in so many ways, something has. Max and Trina open up their home to me for as long as I need. Their couch becomes my new bed; their company becomes my safety net.

I'd started going to therapy back in December, as soon as Nick and I returned from Christmas with my family. He'd come with me for a handful of sessions, but since the crash, I'd gone alone.

"Do you think I should try antidepressants?" I ask my counselor at our next session. On my last phone call with Mom, she'd recommended them, having medicated with them for years herself.

"I've had clients say they help. Considering everything you're going through you may want to give them a try," she says.

The following week, I get a prescription from my doctor.

I wake up in the middle of the night. My body is covered in sweat, my heart pounding out of my chest. I can't catch my breath. The room comes into focus. It's unfamiliar. Disoriented, I try to place myself. *Where am I?* Brown leather couch sticky with sweat. My heart refuses to slow, a jackhammer on overtime. *A heart attack? Oh my God, am I having a heart attack?* I place my hand on my chest. Rapid palpitations reverberate into my palm. *Breathe.* It takes a minute. Slowly, I find it—a sharp, sweet, agonizing inhalation. I come to terms.

I'm not dying . . . at least not right now. It's 2:00 a.m. and I'm wide awake. *A panic attack*, I realize. *The antidepressants I started taking?* Everything that has come undone is catching up, eating away at me from the inside out.

I can't go back to sleep. I toss and turn, restless, miserable, worried about Nick's instability. Thoughts of him and Christine fill my mind. Rage gives way to sadness. Sadness gives way to remembering. I shouldn't, I know it'll only make me feel worse, but my brain is merciless.

I escape from the prison of my blankets and trade them for the prison of my car. Fog has permeated the dark landscape; an eerie quiet fills the streets. My headlights shine into the gray mist. Driving with no destination, crossing bridges, turning down unknown roads, I find myself in a cul-de-sac and pull the parking brake. A light in one of the houses—a large, two-story Colonial—illuminates the living room. On the mantle, photos are displayed. *Do they have children? Are they happy?* I feel a stab of envy. A life I could have lived, a house I could have had, a dream I once thought was mine. Few things can shatter our hearts like expectations.

I don't cry. I can't anymore. I've cried enough for a lifetime and all that is left is numbness. Slumped back into the driver seat, I sit and stare. The car grows icy. Just lifting my arms to the steering wheel feels overwhelming.

After the panic attack, I stop taking the antidepressants. A crushing tidal wave of severe depression sweeps over me and sucks me into its current. The weight of sadness makes it hard to move, to get out of bed. I can't eat, I'm constantly nauseous. The thought of going to work is crippling. The heaviness soaks into my very bones, dragging me into a void of nothingness. Being awake is torment, but every night is long and restless. And I don't want to talk about it, not with anyone. I read somewhere that when pain is not witnessed, we don't feel real. That's me. Empty, hollowed out, inhuman. How long does it take to feel real again? I descend to ash where the only flickering is a few tiny embers glowing faintly from what was once the light of my soul.

⸻

Nick insists on meeting me at the JAG office—the legal support on the military base. He sits idly in the waiting room. When the receptionist calls me back, they won't let him in with me.

"We can only speak to the client who made the appointment . . . Sarah?" Nick grows visibly uncomfortable when I go in alone.

The attorney is a woman in her mid-forties with piercing eyes and gray streaks in her hair. The appointment is brief and she gets right to the point.

"So, will you be requesting spousal support?"

"Spousal support? Like alimony? I thought that was only if you have kids . . . ?" I trail off, feeling ignorant.

She peers at me from across her cluttered desk and shakes her head. "You're entitled to certain financial benefits as part of the divorce process, should you choose to pursue them."

When I tell Nick afterward about the spousal support, he's enraged.

"You could never go through what I've gone through. You would look death in the face and cower. But me? I'm strong. I'm going to overcome this." His eyes cloud with fury as he continues, "We're here because of you! Because of our shitty marriage. That's what pushed me away. It's your fault I even ended up with Christine."

I want to react, but I don't have the energy. We finally agree on a small, one-time payment to help me re-settle in California. My biggest concern is the loan I took out to pay for our wedding. Debt still accruing interest for a strapless white dress I wore once, for gold rings that symbolize nothing, for food scraped into trash cans. A day that once felt like a fairy tale now feels like a giant sham.

"I hope one day you'll help pay it back . . ." I say, trailing off.

"I will," he says quickly, "I promise."

I type up a separation agreement. No children, no shared property. On paper it looks clean, simple, easy. We both sign on the dotted line. In our state of residency, a couple must be separated for several months before they can file for a divorce. The agreement is notarized, and with it, we cross a bridge that crumbles when we step off it.

I think about what leaving him looks like from the outside in. Aside from my family and close friends, no one knows about the affairs, the threats, the depression, just how bad things have become. I imagine people talking back home in our small town: *He almost died in a horrific helicopter crash and she leaves him?! How could she? He needs her now more than ever . . .*

I drown out the voices. I'm as fragile as my world is delicate. Depression has taken my will to care. I can't afford to worry about what anyone thinks or assumes or says. I remind myself that the people who matter will be here for me, no matter what.

Max, Trina, and I find a comfortable routine as roommates. They give me a sense of normalcy in an otherwise catastrophic time. Trina and I continue taking hot yoga classes. The three of us make dinner and watch shows as I play with their pet bunny—ironically named Bear. I continue therapy, where the counselor annoyingly tells me, "You can't control this situation, Sarah, but you can control how you react. Maybe you have more power than you think?"

I head into work downtown and park in the same lot where I had run in alarm after receiving the call from the hospital. I take the elevator to the upper floor, keeping my eyes down. What can I say to these generous people who donated their own time off so I could take care of Nick these past months? I quickly close the door to my office, stand at the floor-to-ceiling window, and gaze out over the cityscape.

In the quiet room, a noise shakes me. A roaring hum. The sound grows louder. I freeze. I know this sound. Then, I see them. Two massive helicopters come into view, the very same kind Nick worked on. *How are they still flying these things?* Tremors pulse through my body, and my knees feel weak.

I catch my desolate reflection in the glass and what I see is startling. A ghost of a girl stares back. Her eyes are hollow; her face is pale. She looks so fragile, so broken. In her shadowed existence, I see the truth—*I can't do this anymore. I can't be here with these constant reminders.* Moving here and building a life was all for Nick. Every road we've been down, every place, every turn reminds me of us. *I have to leave.* It feels like my very life is on the line. What kind of world can I rebuild while being trapped in the past? I can't heal here.

Maybe I do have more power than I thought—the power of choice. Sometimes, endings are the only way to begin again.

14

LEAVING

Extra-large cardboard boxes are piled throughout the living room, the contents of my life thrown haphazardly into each. I'll ship as much as I can back to California and pack the rest in my car. When my mom's name pops up on the phone screen, I swipe to answer. I walk outside into the cool spring air and sit on a bench. It's sunny, the sky a cobalt blue; winter is finally retracting her claws.

"I'm worried about you," she says every time we talk.

Me too, I think. She fills me in on the trip she's taking with my nana next month to Florida. A few days in the Keys, a few days on Sanibel Island.

"That sounds amazing," I tell her. Beaches, warm water, yummy food, family . . . At the thought of family my heart constricts with longing. There's a pause on the other end of the line.

"Sarah?" she asks suddenly. "Why don't you come meet us?"

I think about the boxes piled inside, the job I'm leaving, the life that I know is over. *Why not?* The idea takes hold. *Yes.* For the first time in months, I feel excitement at the prospect of something, *anything*, to get me out of this place. Finally, I have somewhere to go, a direction to look forward to. With it comes hope. Hope is everything.

I lose myself in planning. I notice that I'm sleeping a little better; waking up and getting dressed doesn't require so much energy. I buy my very first pair of hiking boots and plan my route: The Florida Keys and Sanibel with Mom and Nana. New Orleans to visit my brother. Austin for the food and music. Then, to the West. The national parks: Arches, Mesa Verde, Bryce, Zion, the Grand Canyon. The legendary blue of Havasupai. *What better way to start my new life?* The thought of camping, hiking, and backpacking alone gives me pause. *Is it safe? Can I do it?*

I think back to my first (and only) backpacking trip at thirteen—the summer before my freshman year of high school. My two older brothers gave me the lightest pack as we hiked seven miles into pristine Sierra Nevada wilderness. There were crystal-clear alpine lakes, countless stars, crackling campfires. I loved every second. Besides, I'm no stranger to solo travel, having backpacked and lived abroad. Aside from making some pretty questionable decisions, those trips were the most free and alive I'd ever felt. The prospect of reclaiming my once wild and independent spirit is all the motivation I need. I loved that girl, the adventurous one filled with a lust for life.

Camping *alone*, however, will be a totally new experience. Any fears of the *what-ifs* are outweighed by the nightmare of *what's been*. I want desert, mountains, evergreen ceilings, dirt under my feet. "Nature is one of the best remedies for a broken heart," says a pin on my new Pinterest board. Pinterest, like Instagram, is only a few years old. I find inspirational quotes that minister to my heartache and share them to my page, racking up ten likes. Thank God TikTok is years away, otherwise I'd be dancing and crying my way across the country. I post a weep-worthy excerpt from *The Velveteen Rabbit*, say a prayer that nature can heal, and start a hashtag (#sarahhitstheroad).

Leaving my marriage is messy. Loose ends entangle like a snare. I move my belongings out of the apartment, sell our furniture, get a new phone plan, remove my name from the utility bills. Nick asks me to spend a final night with him—his idea of closure. I refuse. Maybe I should be strong enough to let him go without seeing him again, but leaving something like *us* isn't so simple. Desire for finality runs deep. We agree to meet at the local beach one last time to say goodbye.

In classic fashion, I write him a letter. It seems right that where letters had built our relationship, this one will close it. In the envelope, I place my ring and our wedding vows. We sit side by side on the sand, an awkward tension hanging in the salty air.

"Hey," he says quietly.

"Hi . . . This is for you," I say, handing him the envelope. I haven't written kind things, but I have written things that feel true.

"I guess I'll give this back to you," he says, handing me his wedding band. *Is this what divorcing people do?* I wonder. *Give their rings back like something that was simply borrowed for a time?*

The conversation is raw, choked with hurt and the weight of mutual resentment. At one point, Nick takes a selfie—one last picture together. Both our eyes are red, the sadness is real, as is the delusion that it is normal to be capturing this moment. Eventually, I trail off and look out at the ocean. I think about all the memories this beach holds. We took our engagement photos here. Celebrated birthdays. Partied with friends. Just a month ago, I'd come here in the dark of night, running in desperation, screaming at the unforgiving waves while he was seducing another woman.

I look back at Nick. After all that has transpired, the silence speaks the loudest, saying everything and nothing at all.

"Okay... well, I guess I should be going," I say, standing, brushing sand off.

He walks me back to my car and holds the door open as I slide in. Bending down, he kisses the sealed window. My heart beating hard, watching him walk away, I expect him to look over his shoulder. One last glimpse as if to say, *I'll be seeing you*, but he never does. It hits me more than anything. Me sitting there, waiting, expecting.

I turn the key and slowly pull away.

My final days are filled with more goodbyes. I thank the therapist who shifted from trying to save my marriage to trying to save my life. I head into my last day at work where coworkers write sweet farewell cards, give gifts and hugs. I spend an evening with Lori and her family for a farewell dinner. I take my last hot yoga class with Trina. When the time comes to say goodbye to her and Max, it breaks my heart. Trina and I take one too many shots at a honky-tonk. We ride the mechanical bull and decide to get our noses pierced. The state may make me wait to file for a divorce, but I'll be damned if they take away my ability to go *Eat, Pray, Love.* When the sun rises the next morning, Max and Trina walk me to my car. We exchange a final embrace. There are simply no words to convey the place they hold in my heart, all these beautiful people who sheltered me at my darkest.

In my jam-packed Toyota, I pull out of the apartment complex, my headlights revealing the road ahead. As the first rays of sun chase away the dark, I glance into the rearview mirror and feel a surge of sadness. I'm leaving what I thought was my everything behind. Even though I don't want to, I think about the mundane moments Nick and I shared: inside jokes, our love for cute dogs, the trip to Italy we dreamed about, the way he would towel dry my hair after a shower. For whatever reason, here at the end, those small things feel like the significant things. A smudge on the driver's-side window catches my eye—lips—Nick's lips from our last goodbye. A cruel reminder. With a nine-hour drive ahead, the pavement seems relentlessly long. Memories ride shotgun, with only my thoughts to keep me company.

After a long day on the road, I pull up to a campsite on the outskirts of Savannah, Georgia. For the first time in my life, I set up camp on my own. Twisting poles together, I stretch the nylon from each tent corner. As soon as I get one pole in the corner hook, the other falls out. I shimmy from side to side, wedging the tent against a rock, trying to get the poles to stay. After an embarrassingly long struggle, the tent is pitched, the rain cover is on, my sleeping mat and bag unrolled inside. I hang my new hammock between two trees near the water's edge. Perfect. *Now what?* I sigh.

The campground is perched around a large lake. Swans glide in the water. Willow trees around the banks sway gently in the wind. It's peaceful. Quiet. Torturous. The loveliness only amplifies my aloneness. I settle into my hammock and rock with the breeze. I pull out my journal and write:

I know these roads, I've been here before
I know the curves, the bends, the twists
I know this route like the back of my hand
Etched into my mind, I know where not to go
Only because I've been there before
Familiar and comforting, the soft, gentle song
You pull me in and I can't get away
You know my weaknesses, you know my flaws
You've been closer than anyone, seen the very center of my heart
Yet here I am, alone on this shore
And where are you, my love?

You are no more.
Perhaps some roads are better left unexplored.

That night I toss and turn, scared in my tent. Every snap of twigs could be a stranger creeping toward my shelter. Every rustle of the wind hides dark, shadowy things out to get me. Nightmare scenarios play out in my mind. I thought camping alone would be empowering. Instead, I feel vulnerable. And lonely. So achingly lonely. When dawn arrives, I pack up quickly. *Fuck those swans*, I think as I peel out of the campground. The rising sun illuminates the road ahead, yellow lines that stretch into eternity.

Somewhere out there, my new beginning.

PART III
HEALING

15

BEGINNINGS

I drive straight through to the Florida Keys. Nine long hours. The best part of my day is a surprise Starbucks. When it comes to coffee, I'm as hopeless as I was with Nick—that is to say, alarmingly dependent and needy. The lonely hours are a countdown to being with my mom and nana, who arrive in a few days. In the meantime, I'll camp and enjoy one of my favorite places: Bahia Honda State Park.

The sun refracts off the turquoise sea as I walk in the pristine aquamarine. It's bathtub warm and my winter skin happily soaks up the sun. My eyes search the sea floor for conch. They are hard to miss with their big spiral shells, pink underbellies, and unmistakable tracks on the sandy bottom. Bahia has shallow water where one can walk out for what seems like miles. My family had come here on a cross-country motor home trip when I was ten, and I'd snorkeled this beach for hours. I've dreamed of returning ever since.

Thinking back, I shake my head in amazement. A thirty-six-foot RV held eight of us packed in like sardines—six kids and my parents. Behind the rig we towed a Dodge Durango loaded up with kayaks and a heap of bikes. In New Orleans, my dad brazenly drove down narrow cobblestone streets where a drunk observer yelled at us, "Holy shit! Where's your airplane?!" When we arrived in the Florida Keys, I was entranced. This place has happy memories. Maybe, I hope, I can get some of that happiness back.

The lure of what lies underneath the shimmering surface of the water keeps me distracted from my relentlessly questioning mind. *What if I hadn't picked Nick up that night? What if he was going to come back around?* Symbols of purity and power, I like to think that each conch I discover reclaims something that was siphoned away. I attempt exploration like my ten-year-old self—in wonder at the world around her—but I'm left longing for that girl's innocence lost to the tides of time.

Naively, I'd only applied one layer of sunscreen. By mid-afternoon, I'm scorched crimson as a lobster. When Mom and Nana arrive two days later, the burns on my butt are still so severe I can't sit on the toilet without cringing in pain.

Nana sing-songs my voice when I see her. "Is that my Sarah May?"

"Hi, Nana!" I bend down to hug the four-foot, five-inch elegantly dressed, eighty-four-year-old woman before me. With her shock of white curls and sapphire eyes, she effortlessly captures the heart of everyone she meets. I haven't seen Mom since Christmas, and with her embrace, a little piece of me softens.

The mother in front of me is more healed than the mother of my childhood. She's worked hard to face her monsters. Having experienced grace, she offers it in spades. I come to her when I am hurting and she drops everything. We have bonded through honesty and humility. I always knew she loved me, but these days, I feel it like a salve to my spirit. Now, it is her brightness that eclipses my darkness, not the other way around. A vibrant floral dress hangs from her stocky frame. I take her in: gray hair pulled into a ponytail with a bright pink scrunchie, the signature mole on her upper lip, the way her eyes crinkle in the corners like mine. She holds me tight, as if her hug can say just how much she has worried about me, and how happy she is that I'm here, still alive, still breathing.

Mom, Nana, and I form a small legion of three generations prowling the Keys for the best of everything. Over the next week, "the Troops" and I shop, eat Key lime pie, and enjoy the beaches. I swim with dolphins and we visit Ernest Hemingway's house. We tour a shipwreck museum and sample conch fritters. We linger for hours at the butterfly conservancy as hundreds of blue-winged beauties land on our hands and heads. Then, back at Bahia Honda, Mom tries to teach Nana how to snorkel. I take shelter under an umbrella, still nursing candy-apple burns.

Nana waddles to the shoreline in her flippers like an unsteady penguin, but as soon as Mom gets her under the water, a dramatic yelp reaches my ears.

"AAGGHH!" Nana screams through the snorkel and splashes erratically like a fish refusing to be reeled in. Mom tries to steady her and starts to laugh. Her laugh is notoriously high-pitched, a witch-sounding cackle that startles any living thing in the near vicinity. In my self-consumed teenage years, it mortified me—the way people would turn heads and stare when she howled. Once again, her laughter is a showstopper, drawing attention from everyone on the beach.

Nana only panics more. "AAGGHH!"

Now, everyone on the sand is staring in alarm. It looks like Mom is drowning Nana and laughing hysterically while doing it.

Observing the outrageous spectacle, I can no longer contain myself. A giggle escapes my lips. Then . . . a deep, full-bellied laugh. Not like Mom's (*Thank God*), but I laugh so hard I almost pee my bikini. The delightful sound surfaces from deep within. It lights up something that has long been dormant. The reminder of its sweetness makes me want to cry. Mom pulls Nana out of the water, and they shuffle back to the towels, dripping wet, arm in arm, while onlookers resume their beach activities.

The dark clouds around me begin to lighten in the company of this love. I don't talk about anything. I can't yet, and they both give me the courtesy of not asking. Instead, we simply enjoy being together.

In the middle of the night, a buzzing phone wakes me. It's Nick. My heart races. *Why is he calling so late?* The Troops snore away on the other queen bed in our small hotel room. Not wanting to wake them, I tiptoe to the bathroom and swipe to accept his call.

"Nick?" I whisper.

"Sarah . . . you answered." He's drunk, his voice thick, words slurred.

"Nick? It's one in the morning. Is everything okay?"

"No, Sarah. It's not okay. You left me here all alone."

I shouldn't be surprised, but somehow, I still am.

"I was driving . . . There was an accident."

My heart drops. "Oh my God, are you okay? Is anyone hurt? Are you hurt?"

"No. I'm okay. Of course I'm okay, I'm invincible."

"Nick, was anyone else injured? What happened?"

He slurs, "It's fine. You don't need to worry about me anymore."

"Nick, what happened?"

Now that he has my full attention, he takes his time. "I was driving home and I . . . I lost control."

"How fast?" I ask. Not like it matters, it's just the first words that form from my disoriented brain.

"Maybe one hundred and twenty . . . I don't know."

"Nick, you've been drinking!" My voice rises. "You have no business driving. You could have killed yourself! Or someone else!"

He laughs bitterly. An empty, hollow sound. "You don't care. You left me. I'm not your problem. Besides, I'm untouchable."

I try to keep him on the line, assessing if he's physically safe while he babbles about being beyond harm or risk. *At least he's home, and no one is hurt, even if his car is totaled somewhere, unless . . . unless this is all just a ploy to reach out to me . . . to make sure I would answer, to see if I still care?*

"Good night, Sarah. You don't need to worry about me anymore." The line goes flat.

I stand in the bathroom, wide awake, my stomach churning. Forget about sleep. My mind races with worry as the worst-case scenarios play out in my head. This isn't the first time he's done this.

Before I left, he called me late one night and threatened to drive into a tree. In terror, I tried to get through to him, to calm him down. We stayed on the phone until he was safe, but the blame he placed on me was crippling. "This is all your fault," he said. Even as the physical distance between us builds, I worry about his instability, the volatility, the continued threats he makes on his life. The guilt, the manipulation, the worry—when does it end?

The next morning, a text from him lights up my screen.

I want you back. The hope of us getting together is all I'm living for.

A few days later, the sound of steel drums floats over to the Troops and me. A restaurant with live music sits perched on the edge of a beach. We've been exploring Key West all day and are ready to head back to the hotel when Mom exclaims, "Oooh, I love steel drums! Let's go have dinner there!"

We pick our way across the parking lot and give our name for a table on the sand. While we wait, I head inside to order drinks from the bar. Behind the counter, an attractive bartender greets me. His long brown curls are offset by speckled golden-brown eyes. His tan skin and toned muscles pop in his staff T-shirt. His jaw is so chiseled it makes me want to be a sculptor. *Damn.* Instantly, I'm self-conscious.

"Hey," I say casually, "I just want to see about ordering some drinks while we wait." I motion to the Troops outside who are watching me with keen interest.

He smiles, his gaze lingering on mine, making me feel even more exposed. "Are you all waiting for an outdoor table?"

I look away nervously. "Yeah . . ."

He flashes another smile. "Awesome. I'll be your server then . . . That's my section tonight."

I groan inwardly. The Troops are going to have a field day.

"What would you like? I'll bring it out to you."

He appraises me confidently. I hastily order three mojitos and rush outside to gather myself. *Is he flirting with me?* I hadn't been flirted with in so long, let alone remember how to do it myself. *He probably isn't.* I feel so painfully self-conscious that the thought of someone else being interested in me is baffling. I push my thoughts aside as we get seated and he makes his way to our table.

"Hello, ladies. My name is Adrian. I'll be taking care of you tonight."

The Troops are visibly thrilled. If one wants to witness shameless flirtation, I recommend bringing a Nana and Mom along. He sets the mojitos on the table and coos to Nana, "Well, aren't you just lovely. All three of you, how special to all be together. Where are you ladies from?"

As they swoon, I watch the exchange with amusement. He catches my eye and we hold our gaze a moment too long. The second he leaves, the Troops excitedly whisper, "Well . . . he's gorgeous, isn't he, Sarah? And so charming!"

And he was. This was going to be a long dinner. I reach for my mojito and gulp it down. The three of us drink, talk, and laugh, enjoying the sounds of the drums as the sun sets over Key West. Every time Adrian stops by the table, the exchanges become livelier, his flirting more overt as the Troops encourage the progression. With some liquid courage, I engage back. It feels awkward, wrong even. But I'm single now, I remind myself. *Single.* That word is still so foreign. Adrian continues the playfulness. He's light, fun. His smile and laugh are contagious, and soon an energy builds between us.

I realize I'd forgotten what it was like to be flirted with, how good it feels to be desired. The more I drink, the less self-conscious I become. As the night progresses, so too does the now-palpable chemistry between us.

Tipsy, I excuse myself to the bathroom. When I return, Mom excitedly gives me the report. "Okay, as soon as you left, he came up to us and told us how beautiful you are." I roll my eyes. She continues, "Then he asked us what your deal is."

"Well . . . what did you say?"

She smiles coyly. "I told him you just went through a really terrible breakup and you know what he said? He said that he's sorry to hear it, but that it's lucky for him." Her eyes gleam. My stomach flip-flops. *Mom . . . the ultimate wing-woman.*

He returns to the table a few minutes later, continuing his repertoire of jokes as the Troops laugh.

"They love you!" I say.

"And you don't?" he teases, gently placing a hand on my arm. Blushing, I play along.

As dinner concludes, my tipsy brain wonders, *How does this end?*

I consult the Troops. "What do you think, should I leave my number?"

Their eyes glow with the fun of it all. "Ummm, of course!" Mom practically shouts.

I consider. *Why not?* For the first time in my life, I scribble down my number and hand it to him when he drops off the check. He smiles at me and winks. He had the same idea. On the check he wrote:

Let's keep this going, call me – Adrian.

My face flushes when we say our goodbyes. He hugs us one by one, and I pluck up the courage to kiss him on the cheek.

In the car ride back to the hotel, my blood is on fire with rum, my mind racing with images of Adrian. I'm silent in the back seat. Something is reawakened. Something I haven't felt in longer than I can remember. I can't recall the last time Nick flirted with me, even playfully. After hearing him tell me he was assessing other women, wondering if he could get with them, experiencing betrayal not just once, but multiple times, my self-esteem had been slowly and painfully dismantled. At dinner I could hardly believe what was transpiring. That this gorgeous guy would be interested in me?

I replay the interactions with Adrian in my head. I see his amber eyes, his smile; I feel his touch and for the first time in what seems like a lifetime, I feel butterflies.

Not ten minutes after leaving, a text lights up my screen:

Sarah, it's Adrian. What are you doing tonight? I get off in 30. Want to meet? I'd love to see you again.

Tonight? So soon? What will the Troops say? I find the nerve to ask their advice, and they practically push me out of the car.

"Go! Go have fun!"

I'm momentarily shocked. Here is my Christian mother telling me to go meet the smoking hot bartender and my eighty-four-year-old nana nodding vigorously beside her.

Apparently, they know what I would soon learn: that sometimes, after immeasurable darkness, it's okay to let in the light. It's okay to be reminded of what it feels like to be wanted, to laugh and have fun. More importantly, it was okay to grant myself permission to do so. The road to recovery is as individual and subjective as it is unpredictable and surprising. Letting someone in can be just as much a remedy as letting someone go.

I want to know what it's like to be held tight after being pushed away. I want to know what it feels like to be with someone else. Someone who will look at me with hungry eyes and open arms and who will care about my pleasure. I don't think about whether or not I'm "ready." In fact, I'm not sure what that even means. So, I just do it. Without another thought about what Nick would say or do, I shower and change.

Thirty minutes later, I go meet a man who made me feel something I'd long forgotten. And when we kiss for the first time—my first non-Nick kiss in years—it's like learning how to do it all over again, because in so many ways, I am learning how to do everything all over again. I am beginning again. So, I give myself this gift. For the next few days, I let in the light.

I decide one thing: *I will be unapologetic about my healing journey.*

16

ROAD TRIP

Mama becomes my road trip copilot. She packs her bag into my already crammed car for the next week. At first, I'm apprehensive about the time together—hours on end in a tiny hatchback? Then, I recall the routine nightmare fest sleeping in my tent, the lonely stretches of road where my thoughts ran wild. Being with the Troops was a good distraction. Alone still feels too daunting. We route the GPS to New Orleans, load up on Starbucks double shots, and put Florida in the rearview.

After a thirteen-hour drive across four state lines, Mom and I are delirious from listening to one too many books on tape. We pull up to my brother's studio near the Garden District. Aaron greets us at the door of his quaint shotgun-style apartment with open arms. A wide grin consumes his face. Bald, with a dark brown beard, he looks every part of the hippie artist that he is, barefoot in cutoff jean shorts and a ripped-up tee.

I was born on Aaron's second birthday. Not wanting his special day to be overshadowed, Mom told him, "Sarah is your birthday present from Jesus." He took it to heart.

Whenever people tried to hold me or fawn over the new baby, he'd push their hands away, saying, "Mine, mine." Over the years, we've drifted in and out of being best friends to keeping our respective secrets.

I'd called all my siblings when I decided to leave Nick and shared news of our separation. "He cheated," was all I could say. Emotionally, I was numb. I still am.

Over pizza and beer, Aaron and I reconnect in his backyard. The humidity is thick; crickets buzz in sparse grass. The little I disclose comes from a detached place.

"I tried. I tried so hard," I say, not needing to explain myself at all.

Tears well in Aaron's eyes as he shakes his head in anger. "I'm so sorry, Sarah. I can't imagine how painful this has been. It makes me so mad."

"I know," I acknowledge softly.

The sting of betrayal isn't reserved solely for me. My family had embraced Nick into the fold. He'd charmed his way in with humor and gifts, over drinks with siblings, and heartfelt conversations with my parents. There are shared memories and experiences that will forevermore bear his presence. No one would feel the pain as much as my youngest brother. He and Nick were thick as thieves. When my marriage came undone, he'd felt personally betrayed. By choosing Nick, I hadn't just hurt myself, I'd hurt my family too. *I'm sorry*, I want to tell everyone. I brought Nick into all our lives. I asked them to love him, to welcome him, to stand by us in marriage . . . and now, I'm asking them to cut him out. They'll do it, but years from now, will they trust me when I ask them to open their hearts to someone else all over again? I still haven't found the words to explain the darkness I've been fumbling through. But with someone like Aaron, I don't have to.

"Go get dressed in something nice," he tells me.

"What for?" I ask.

"Just do it, you'll see," he says, winking at Mom and pushing me playfully toward the door.

I change just in time for the surprise to be revealed. Aaron has orchestrated a girls' night out, enlisting his female friends with the sole mission of having fun and cheering me up. He'd even prepaid for the taxi and a round of drinks at a swanky bar. I'm beyond touched by his thoughtfulness.

"Do me a favor," he says, "go have fun tonight. Let loose. Enjoy yourself."

He wraps me in a hug. In his embrace—just as with my mom's—I am reminded that love doesn't care where you've been or what you've done or what has happened to you. Love says, *I'm with you*. I look at Aaron and Mom and I know, unequivocally, that these beautiful people are with me. After feeling the heartrending, aching depths of pain, I know that I am not alone.

The next night, somewhat recovered from my girls-gone-wild revelry (I may have strutted down Bourbon Street wielding a cane like a baton), I lie on an air mattress in Aaron's living room where my thoughts turn to Nick. After his message about us getting back together, I'd texted him that we would talk later, but when? The truth is, I don't want to. I know where the conversation will lead, the way I'll feel—emptied out, exhausted—and more than anything, what's the point? With space comes perspective.

I had done my best to be patient and compassionate with Nick. He always said no one could ever understand what he was going through as an excuse to be angry at the world, to justify his behavior. I wasn't on that helicopter. I couldn't possibly know his pain and suffering. But it strikes me that after a disaster, a crisis, a tragedy, we are forever changed. There's no going back. At some point, we have to choose:

What now? How will I move on from this? I don't blame him for his grief or depression or anger, but I do hold him accountable for his behavior. I hold him accountable because he chose to be a victim. I know this because I had too.

Driven by the need to do something, *anything*, to put distance between myself and the man I knew, the life I had, I pull up my social media account. All the memories together, all the photos of Nick and me. I pause in the dark. Debating. My finger hovers over a photo of us.

Delete.

I feel guilty. *Why?* At the same time, it hurts too much to have them there. They feel like a lie. I don't want to see them, don't want to be reminded. I need more than just physical distance.

Delete.

The memories disappear, one by one, my finger hovering before I let each go. The concerts, the parties, the trips, the birthdays, the celebrations. Our wedding.

Delete.

From the outside looking in, it would appear that overnight, the last three years never happened. Just like that, all traces of Nick are gone. Except, erasing such a deep loss isn't so simple. While I can make it look like I'm no longer his, I know better. The traces that matter most are the wounds carried in the heart, the ones it feels like I will always carry.

⁓

Near Austin, Texas, is a quaint state park with a campground. A rushing creek runs through its borders; trees line the water's edge. Mom and I set up camp, then take turns reading out loud and lounging in the hammock. At night, we barely squeeze inside the backpacking tent meant for a solo traveler. The stars come out as wind rustles through cottonwoods. Within minutes, Mom is snoring. Even though the sound keeps me awake, I look at her nestled in a sleeping bag and my heart swells. *Here's a sixty-two-year-old woman sleeping on the hard ground in a ridiculously tiny tent because she didn't want me to be alone.*

Years later, Mom will tell me, "I was so worried about you that whole time. I knew you were ready to leave Nick, and then the crash happened and I thought, well shit . . . she can't leave him now." She was never disappointed in me for staying, just as she was never judgmental of me for leaving. My mom was always rooting for me. She only wanted me to be happy, even if it meant letting me backpack Europe by myself at sixteen, stand at the altar at twenty-one, and file for divorce at twenty-three. Her love looked like uncomfortable nights and long drives and putting up with me in my self-absorbed state. My mom wasn't perfect, but she showed up when I needed her the most and that, to me, means everything.

I wish I could know that one day I will look back on this trip together as infinitely precious. That when the time comes when I don't have my mom, my heart will ache from the inside out, longing for one more cackle, one more song belted out together, one more conversation, one more moment where I can hear her snore and think: *You're so annoying and I love you so much and I don't know what to do in a world without you.*

But here, now, in this moment, I drift off to sleep with my mama, my copilot, my cheerleader beside me as the stars gleam above.

17
THE COMPANY I KEEP

I say farewell to my travel companion at the Salt Lake City airport. In one week, Mom and I had traversed 2,600 miles and spent fifty hours on the open road together. Over the course of seven days, we made memories that only a long road trip can create. I navigated to the sound of her voice as she read to me, counting down miles with music and audiobooks. We sang along to the *Pitch Perfect* soundtrack at the top of our lungs and snuck wine into the jacuzzi at the KOA. We bought matching turquoise rings and meandered through Southwest towns. We explored Mesa Verde, climbing through cliff dwellings and marveling at petroglyphs. She woke me up in the cramped tent by singing oldies and flicking the condensed moisture in my face. Sometimes she tried to talk about Nick, to draw me out emotionally. But mostly, the trip was full of soft, sweet moments where she sat with me and we didn't need to say a word.

I squeeze her tight as I drop her off at the curb.

"Be safe," she tells me.

"I will," I promise, kissing her cheek.

I feel ready for my solo adventure. Being alone no longer seems so daunting, so torturous. If anything, I'm excited. I wave goodbye and set my sights on Southern Utah.

∽

I shiver in the flimsy tent, peering out the door where snowflakes fall in the darkness. The cold penetrates every layer of clothing. My fire, dwindling to embers, had done nothing to alleviate the chill. The cheap sleeping bag I'd purchased is thin, meant for warmer weather. Bryce Canyon National Park is about 8,000 feet above sea level, and the weather in May can swing rapidly. I curse myself for not being more prepared and consider sleeping in the car. Resigned, I miserably curl up.

The morning light is a welcome relief when it chases away the dark and melts the little snow that has accumulated. Among towering pines, I lace up my hiking boots and shoulder my backpack. Fairyland Loop offers an eight-mile trek through the park. Warily, I regard the sign that cautions of mountain lion attacks. Even more warily, I read the info marker and consider what kind of person was able to fight one off using nothing but a ballpoint pen. *New nightmare unlocked.*

An icy blast cuts through my layers. I check the temperature; with the wind chill my phone says seventeen degrees. I understand why Elizabeth Gilbert chose Italy, India, Bali. Those places are generally warm and exotic. So far, my *Eat, Pray, Love* equivalent is freezing with a chance of being eaten. I put one foot in front of the other, losing myself in my thoughts.

I marvel at the famous hoodoos, whimsy auburn towers of sandstone sculpted through the eons by water. Gnarled piñons and junipers scent the air. The open sky is baby blue; tufts of clouds fly with the wind. Miles pass without seeing another hiker. The wilderness serves as a springboard: *When had I really given myself time to be alone?* For so long it was too painful, too terrifying. I needed the anchor of others, a safety net. Now, out here, there is nothing else to distract me and nowhere else to look. I come face-to-face with *me*. In some ways, it's a more terrifying prospect than a cougar—confronting what I've been avoiding.

Do I even know who I am anymore? I'd invested everything into my relationship, devoting all my energy to being a good wife. I thought that was what marriage required, putting the other selflessly before the self. Nick always came first. Even if it was at great self-expense. It occurs to me that perhaps the gravest and most tragic thing of all was not that I lost my *husband*, it was that I'd slowly and surely lost *myself*.

I became so removed from *me* that I had trouble even knowing who I was apart from *him*. I was so dependent on him and our relationship for meaning in my life, I'd lost sight of the shores of my own knowing. I recall my sister telling me months before the wedding, "Nick doesn't seem to know himself at all." I'd denied it vehemently and shrugged her off, because now I realize the implication: What did that mean about me?

The path ahead means rediscovering who I am apart from a man and a marriage. With each step, I imagine leaving it all behind, shedding who I was. What remains? Rather, *who remains?* Thankfully, I have markers to follow.

I love campfires. And s'mores. Stargazing. The smell of rain falling on dry earth. Coffee, hot yoga, dancing. My family's silly annual lip-sync competition. Sourdough. God, I love sourdough. A steaming hot shower. A really good laugh. The list evolves. *The wonder of holding my nieces and nephews in my arms for the first time. The audacity to take this trip when I felt so broken. That my longing for adventure is still alive after all.*

So many beautiful things rise to the surface. Gratitude lightens my step. There is so much to love about life; it just takes looking.

It was love that helped me leave, in the hearts and minds of the people I said goodbye to. It wrapped me up and held me tight in the Florida Keys. It filled the spaces of things unspoken between my mother, brother, and me. This morning, I'd tied the laces of my hiking boots with it and braided my hair with it. Even more love is waiting for me in the arms of family and friends back in California. And there is love here, alone in Bryce, driving me forward. Perhaps the road ahead will not be as long as I feared. Maybe making my way back to myself begins with the things I love and ends when I have reclaimed all the pieces.

I take in the beauty around me: mounds of rock sculpted by time, rich colors so vivid they beg to be painted, trees dancing in the wind, sunlight filtering through their grasp. And *me*. I include myself, for the first time, in the inventory of beautiful things to behold. I'd found the courage and strength to leave. Maybe it took longer than it should have, but it took what it took. For so long, I'd looked to Nick to save me. When everything came undone, I had to save myself. Worth, I realize, is the removal of oneself from a harmful situation for the sanctity of oneself.

Here, in the back country, on the winding trails of Bryce, I find something true. Something that can't be stolen or destroyed or betrayed. Following the cairns that had been hidden deep within, I shake off the bonds of a self-inflicted slumber. I peel my eyes open to find the sun shining, a new day beckoning. Right here, right now, I'm proving to myself what kind of woman I want to be. Held together by what she loves, not by what she lacks. I can hike, camp, and backpack alone. I can even enjoy the solitude. I can learn to like the company I keep when there is no one around. I respect the woman who chose this new beginning. A woman who is slowly learning to be enough, all on her own.

18

WORTH

The glow of the headlamp illuminates my breath as I disconnect tent poles with numb fingers. Tossing the remaining gear into the back of my car, I'm ready to depart for warmer weather at a lower altitude. Zion National Park awaits, a short drive away. I thaw out with the heater and say a prayer of thanks that I didn't freeze to death or get eaten by a wild cougar. *So far, so good.*

I sit in a line of thirty cars for the first-come, first-serve camp spots inside the park boundary. Luck is on my side. I claim a spot right next to the Virgin River, a small but mighty cascade that courses around boulders, roots, and dislodged trees, creating a symphony of babble; the same force carved the marvel of Zion over millions of years. After setting up camp, I venture out to explore the park's attractions—towering vermilion rock walls, meandering canyons, alluring waterfalls. I pick my way up the chain on Angels Landing, don waterproof garb to wade through the Narrows, and take in sweeping views with pesky chipmunks at Observation Point. Then, on my last night in the park, I meet the Aussies. Four charming, handsome men with irresistible accents who invite me to join them at their campfire. *Yes, please.*

We sit around the flames, chatting, when one prods, "Drop bears... you've never heard of 'em?"

I shake my head no.

"Oh yeah, they're all over Aussie land. They hang out in trees, up in the branches, and when something walks underneath... BOOM!" he shouts so loud I jump. "They drop on their prey. You have to be careful walking around the forest, or else you might get dropped on."

I laugh. "No way, you're messing with me."

One of the others chimes in, "It's true, we just don't tell a lot of people about it. We don't want to scare away the tourists. It's like a locals-only thing."

Still shaking my head, I roll my eyes as they continue to challenge me. Their steadfastness makes me doubt myself. I take a mental note to google "drop bears" as soon as I have service.

The fire crackles as we sit and share stories over beer and the overpriced box of Cheez-Its purchased at the nearby market. The stars come out as the night deepens over our conversation of travel, books, Vegemite, and hiking. When the flames dwindle, I take my leave and walk back to my tent. After I settle into my sleeping bag, a voice startles me.

"Sarah, are you awake?"

It's one of the Aussies. I mumble that I am.

"I figured I'd come by and check on ya, to see if you're lonely. You want some company in there?"

Truthfully, I didn't. I was tired and buzzed and he was definitely drunk. At the same time, while I didn't mind being alone, I also didn't want to be.

"Sure," I say groggily, unzipping my tent just enough to let him in. My heart knew better, but my lips said yes. What follows isn't satisfying as we fumble in the dark. When he finally leaves and I lie awake, alone in my tent, shame washes over me. *Why did I do that?* I toss and turn, sick of myself and guilt-ridden. Self-deprecating thoughts eat away at me into the early hours of the morning.

The next day, I pack up camp early so I don't have to see the Aussies again. Setting out on the trail, I feel like I was squashed by a drop bear—an overwhelming concoction of exhaustion, humiliation, and hangover keeps me self-absorbed. My head hanging low, I avert my gaze from other hikers. *Why did it feel so different hooking up with Adrian? It was essentially the same thing, wasn't it?* I have a hard time reconciling the two. Shame does that—incapacitating with its grip, confining in silence, convincing in its righteousness. My newfound confidence, fragile to begin with, fades. I outsourced something precious and am left with a defeating inner monologue that validates my deepest insecurities.

As I put the miles behind me and the silence gives me space to think, I realize that when I said *Sure* to the Aussie, I hadn't meant it. I'd left my marriage feeling painfully undesirable and inadequate. Feeling wanted is a slippery slope in my recuperating heart. Having my sense of self-worth attached to someone else *feels familiar.*

I recall a book on codependence my sister sent me when Nick and I first started dating. At the time, I was annoyed. I thought, *She just doesn't understand us.* Because someone who had known me all my life and was a trained clinical therapist couldn't possibly understand, right?

When I eventually reread the book, it will strike a chord. In my refusal to see our dysfunction at the time, I became a co-creator in a relationship that was wildly unhealthy. When I'm honest with myself, it's all too glaringly true to deny.

While codependence was originally coined to apply to partners of addicts, the term has since expanded. Dr. Nicole LePera defines codependence as "the chronic neglect of self in order to gain approval, love, validation, or self-identity through another person."

Melody Beattie, author of *Codependent No More*, writes that: "Codependency is many things. It's a dependency on people—on their moods, behaviors, sickness or well-being, and their love."[1]

When I read about the characteristics of a codependent, I uncomfortably acknowledge aspects of myself in every single one:

Caretaker—*to the core*. Low self-worth—*definitely*. Obsession—*both with him and our relationship, yes*. Controlling—*the queen*. Trouble communicating needs—*I usually don't even know what mine are . . . so, yeah* (another codependent trait). Weak boundaries—*obviously*. Needed him rather than wanted him—*double yes*. Believed his lies, lied to protect him, lied to myself—*so many times I lost count*. Self-sacrificed to the point of resentment—*all the freaking time*.

Clarissa Pinkola Estés writes in *Women Who Run with the Wolves*, "We all have made the mistake of thinking someone else can be our healer, our thriller, our filling. It takes a long time to find it isn't so, mostly because we project the wound outside ourselves instead of ministering to it within."[2] It's clear that I projected my wounds and looked outside of myself for the validation of being enough, unknowingly begging for someone else to make me whole.

Love was being needed. Rescuing made me feel indispensable. I chose from a place of inadequacy and was hooked through my sickness to someone who was incapable of ever giving me what I desperately sought. Nick's behavior was a reflection of the valuation of my self-worth, so how he felt about me became how I felt about me. Because my identity was so wrapped up in him, when he betrayed me, it was the equivalent of shattering me into a million pieces, as if to say I wasn't enough. I tolerated abuse to keep what we called love.

I think about all the red flags and warning signs dismissed in the name of being swept away in our shiny infatuation. The infidelity long before we said I do. The weekly screaming matches that lasted hours, their climax that left me hyperventilating while Nick mocked my constricted sobs. The time he drunkenly shoved me up against the wall in a jealous rage after accusing me of flirting with his friend, pinning me in place, his face bloodshot, spit flying from his mouth, the stench of alcohol. The time he slammed his wedding ring in my chest and threatened to tear up our marriage certificate. Once, intoxicated, I shoved Nick hard for appearing to flirt with an attractive coworker.

The fights were so vicious we decided only one of us would drink if we went out. Nick would often get drunk while I stayed sober. I think of all the times I filled the role of mother more than wife, waking up early to make him breakfast and lunch. Coming home from work to grocery shop, make his dinner, do laundry, and clean the apartment. When he enrolled in online courses, I even did his homework when he claimed it was "too much." I surrendered on issues I once felt strongly against, like buying a gun and getting a concealed carry permit. I even stopped being a vegetarian. All to make him happy. Codependent—*Who, me?*

The intensity of our mutual inadequacy became passion. It was "us against the world" when, in actuality, it was us against ourselves. He was my other half, my missing piece, my completion. We normalized it to the point of idealizing it. I thought he'd saved me, that I'd saved him, but salvation is never found in another. Redemption is an inside job.

The realization makes me sick, the weight of truth heavy to confront. Underneath the layers of what I thought was love, I gave him all of me, thinking he was my everything, and the cost almost *was* everything.

In the face of this overwhelming evidence, I consult an internal jury. I tolerated so much harm, creating a prison of my own enabling. From little ways to monumental compromises, my codependence was a glue that held us together. It hurts to admit it, to own the sickness within myself. But after sitting in the cell long enough, I discover I also have the key.

Melody Beattie, again, writes: "One day the truth caught up to us and refused to be put off any longer. This wasn't what we wanted, planned on, asked for, or hoped for. It never would be. The dream was dead, and it would never breathe again."[1]

That dream was not only my marriage but a hauntingly false sense of self and a way of being in relationship that was wholly destructive and harmful. I feel acutely understood, yet grossly implicated. All this time, I'd painted Nick as the sole perpetrator, the guilty one, the offender. In so many ways he was, but what *I* had done for love was also deeply wounding.

After the Aussie hookup, I begin to understand that reconnecting to worthiness is critical. Through painful self-inquiry, I see where I'm susceptible. When I'm honest about the way last night's fling leaves me feeling, I decide guilt is a better teacher than shame. Shame leaves no space for grace. Guilt can motivate one to choose differently. While being with Adrian was a reminder of what I deserve, being with the Aussie was unwanted, unsatisfying, and, ultimately, a self-betrayal.

It's a lesson I'll learn many times over. It won't be my last guilt-inducing hookup. There is a critical difference between saying *yes*, knowing my worth, and exploring pleasure from a healthy place and it contrasts sharply with what happened last night. For much of my life, I haven't known that difference. My self-esteem has been largely dictated by external validation. Receiving male attention has been the flawed metric by which I've long measured enoughness. Feeling wanted is a desperation in my yearning heart that only points her finger back at me.

What was familiar before would now need to become a stranger. The ambivalence I had felt in saying *sure* was actually *no*. I have a long way to go as I take responsibility for my choices. Whenever there is a lure of feeling wanted at the expense of self, I decide to choose a new way. A way that doesn't require harm or betrayal. I know the cost, and it is too great.

I stop by the side of the hiking trail. I stare down at red rock earth beneath my dusty boots and take a deep breath. I choose to forgive myself. I remember that I'm relearning how to be. I'll make mistakes, probably many more. It has to be okay. All I can do is try to learn from each one, to offer myself grace and try to do better. I'll build myself into the woman I know I'm capable of being: confident, discerning, healthy. I lift my gaze and trek on.

As soon as I get back into town and have cell phone service, I google "drop bears." I laugh out loud as my eye catches the very first search result: *A fictional creature . . . a hoax in contemporary Australian folklore . . . commonly spoken about in tall tales to scare tourists.* I roll my eyes, putting Zion and the Aussies behind me as I set out for my next adventure.

19
STRENGTH

On a shuttle to the trailhead, I trace my route on the Grand Canyon National Park map: down the South Kaibab Trail, a steep seven-mile descent into the heart of the canyon, follow the Colorado River for a few miles, then begin the arduous, switchback ascent via the Bright Angel Trail for a final nine-mile trek back to the rim. Over seventeen miles. A knee-pounding five thousand feet down, then five thousand feet of climbing right back up. I figure this last stretch will feel like an eternity. The Park Service advises people *not* to make the hike in a single day. Multiple visitors a year have to be rescued from the canyon due to heatstroke, dehydration, and injury. Some even go missing, having fallen to their death with a misstep or losing their balance as they take a selfie. Of all the ways to die.

I heard about the ambitious challenge to hike in and out of the Grand Canyon in a single day just a week ago—my neighbor at the Bryce campground, a forty-year-old solo female traveler, had intrigued me with the story of her accomplishment. She'd inspired me. I naively thought to myself: *I'm in good shape, my boots are broken in. What better way to feel strong and empowered?* (Please, take the Park Service more seriously than me.)

I jump off the shuttle, adjust my pack, and take a moment to appreciate the view. Layer after layer of crimson rock descends into the depths of the canyon and stretches to a saphire horizon. The early morning sun casts long shadows across eroded strata. Junipers line the trail. This isn't my first awe-inspiring sight of the park. My family had come here on our cross-country RV trip, only we'd visited the North Rim post-blizzard. All was silent, frozen over. Snow capping the red rocks was a magical sight, but I was too young to appreciate the vastness. In such a grand place, it's impossible not to feel small. Shifting my eyes from the landscape, I take a few safe selfies and hike on.

A relentless sun shines down; heat reflects from the stones scattering the trail. Clouds of dust rise with little poofs every step I take, coating my boots in a thick layer. With my shirt, I wipe the sweat from my neck. The temperature this time of year can swing severely. At the rim it's in the mid-sixties, but at the Colorado River it could be thirty degrees warmer. The mighty snaking force that created this spectacle beckons far below. South Kaibab Trail is infamously steep, with 22 percent grade in some places. My knees are already resentful as I pick my way down, mile by mile. I can't help but wonder how the hell it'll feel climbing back up. I take a big swig of water and adjust my hat. Up ahead, I hear the now familiar sound of donkeys braying. A trail guide leads a pack of mules back up to the rim.

As I hike, an Indian man in his mid-forties speeds up after I pass him. From behind, he asks, "Are you alone?"

I slow and half turn, making brief eye contact. "Yep, going it solo."

This curiosity from strangers has become all too familiar. In the past few parks, I've experienced all kinds of interest in me and my trip as a young woman, some genuinely kind and harmless, some not. Sensing that this guy is in the first category, we strike up a brief conversation. I tell him of my plans to hike in and out over the next few hours. Visibly impressed, he tells me, "You know, some people run from rim to rim and back in a day, over forty-eight miles!"

I raise my eyebrows, gazing down at the ever-unfolding precipice. "And I thought I was crazy! It's difficult enough to hike!" I exclaim, as we both shake our heads.

Our conversation dwindles, my pace outmatching his. He smiles. "Well, this is where I leave you. Best of luck!"

Alone, I lose myself in my thoughts, stopping occasionally for a photo. I think back to that morning. I'd been waiting in a long line of cars at the entrance, anxious to begin my hike. My favorite album, Lord Huron's *Lonesome Dreams*, played from the stereo, the lyrics to "Ends of the Earth" floating through the car. Seemingly out of nowhere, I began to cry. I cried so hard my vision blurred and the bumper ahead grew hazy. I couldn't stop the flow. Just like in the yoga class, it was cathartic, liberating, and wholly unexpected. I realized it was the first time I'd cried, really cried, since leaving the East Coast. It marked a sharp contrast for someone who could barely *stop* crying before. The numbness was slowly beginning to dissipate. The why, the when, the how, they rarely seem to matter—the heart has her own timeline. For whatever reason, on my way to that sprawling chasm of rocks and spires, out in the far reaches of Arizona, emotions had surfaced. I cried out of sadness. I cried out of a relief that I was just beginning to understand. Self-conscious the strangers creeping in line beside me might be alarmed by a girl sobbing hysterically over the steering wheel, I pulled down my sunglasses and let the tears flow. Water in the desert.

When I arrive at the Colorado River, the brown, silty cascade is a welcome sight. A rafting excursion readies for departure on a sandy bank. I restock my water, strip some layers, down a quick lunch, and hurry back onto the trail, the sweat stains on my T-shirt still damp. *The ascent. Here we go.*

As I push onward, I pass a man in his mid-thirties sitting on a ledge, wearing running garb and a camelback. His tall, lean frame is contoured by tight, athletic gear. We exchange hellos. A mile or so later, footsteps pound behind me. I quickly move to the side and watch in awe as trail runners raise a cloud of dust, leaving me in their wake. The same man passes with another wave.

The miles dwindle, much slower now. I glance up at the endless switchbacks, a taunting zigzag straight up the canyon wall. *I can do this.* My thoughts turn to a quote I saw scrolling on Pinterest in my tent last night: "If you can love the wrong person that much, imagine how much you can love the right one." *Had I chosen the wrong person?* My confidence to know what the *right* decision is feels shattered. This trip, being alone, hiking absurd amounts, how much of it is to prove to myself that I *can* trust me, that I'm strong enough on my own? All I know is that if I endured so much for someone else, I can endure a hell of a lot more for me. Every step serves as confirmation. Here I am, sweaty, exhausted, but relentless. Putting mile after brutal mile behind me in the most dramatic gorge in the world.

Again, I pass the ultra-runner from earlier. He stands to the side of the trail, catching his breath. This time when I walk by, he keeps up with me.

"Hiking alone?" he says with a grin that has kindness written all over it.

Once again, I confirm. Still in disbelief, I ask him, "Are you really running the entire canyon?"

His smile falters. "I'm attempting to." He'd thrown up at the river and lost a few toenails along the way. *And I thought I was hardcore.* We idly converse as we hike. He's here with a group of friends, all ultra-runners, some of them ranked the best in the world. "You hike fast," he observes. "Want some company?"

"Umm, I don't want to hold you back."

"Not at all. It would be a welcome distraction. The only thing is . . . I shouldn't stop moving or my muscles will spasm. So, if you stop, I'll just run in circles around you."

I raise my eyebrows and peer up at the sheer cliff before us. I stifle a laugh at the absurdity of him running circles around me, but nod anyway. Soon, one of his running buddies joins us and the three of us chat up long inclines as they jog beside me. The miles pass a little more quickly now that I have company. The sun sinks lower and lower on the horizon. Sometimes it's nice to not have to go it alone, even if we know that we can.

A few hours later, we climb the last series of switchbacks as the top of Bright Angel comes into view. I press on, elated, feeling a new burst of energy despite my aching body. I offer to my new friends, "Please don't feel like you need to stay with me if you want to run the final leg."

They both shake their heads. "No way. We're in this together!"

We crest the final ridge, our jubilation rising. After seventeen miles, seven hours, and 10,000 feet of bone-jarring hiking, we ascend to the top of the South Rim. Each of us lets out a glorious holler. Triumphant, I can't stop grinning. I hug my new friends as we capture the moment with a photo. Even though I'm exhausted, my legs trembling, stomach rumbling, a sense of pride swells within. *I did it.* Instead of feeling small in the midst of something so grand, I feel expansive.

The ultra-runner asks for my number. "You should meet up with us tomorrow," he says hopefully. I know that I won't, the recent lesson from my Aussie hookup still fresh. No unzipping my tent, no changing course for someone else. We say goodbye as the sun sets and I board the shuttle back to my car. I glance at the canyon one last time. Farewell for now.

On the bus, I look at the picture we snapped. As I stare at the girl in the photograph, I feel a sense of awe. Just months earlier, she'd been half alive. Barely eating, hardly sleeping, numbly struggling through the day. Now, her eyes are vibrant, her smile glows, her shirt is sweat-stained, but she's magnetic. She's proved to herself something that seemed unimaginable before: She can overcome; she has what it takes.

Resilience comes from the inside out when we make the choice to be greater than our suffering, to face down the darkness. While someone else can make us feel less than, ultimately we are stronger than the worst thing that has ever happened to us. After all, we're still here. Huffing for air, climbing the cliff, putting one foot in front of the other, one ass-kicking mile at a time. Maybe we vomit along the way or lose a few toenails. But we persevere. We find our footing. Hopefully, we don't tumble off the edge taking a stupid selfie.

I close my eyes and hold onto this sweet moment. Stinky and sweaty, sitting next to strangers on a cramped, bumpy bus. There is no one to celebrate me but me, and somehow, that is more than enough.

20

BY THE LIGHT OF THE MOON

I groan as I wiggle out of the sleeping bag, my muscles screaming, *What have you done?!* My entire body aches, and the blisters on my feet are raw. Little do they know they are in for another adventure. Today, I embark on my first solo backpacking trip.

Backpacking, where people prove their mettle by being completely self-sufficient in the wilderness. How it looks? Badass. How it feels? TBD. The implication: It means carrying *everything*. And to do it alone means no one else can help shoulder the burden, quite literally.

It's only ten miles, I reason overconfidently. *I've backpacked before*. Once. I've backpacked before once. And I was thirteen. And my brothers basically carried everything. So yeah . . . This should be good.

I pack up my trunk and head south to the Havasupai Indian Reservation. Briefly, I wonder if I'm overdoing it. Less than twenty-four hours ago, I'd hiked rim to river to rim of the Grand Canyon, and in another few short hours I'll be attempting a trek to the legendary turquoise waterfalls of Havasupai . . . with the weight of a small child strapped to my back. I had barely managed to secure a reservation—the famous attraction requires a permit from the local

Indigenous tribe, and to snag one is a feat in and of itself. I called every day for weeks checking for cancellations. To my delight, someone had opted out of their stay. The prospect of *not going* isn't even a consideration. Some sore muscles won't stop me. My inflated ego agrees enthusiastically.

An assortment of vehicles occupies the trailhead parking lot. Already, there are masses of people swarming about. For hikers who prefer to be packless, they can pay to have mules take their gear to Supai village. For those not interested in long, hot, dusty trails, they can fly. The whir of helicopter blades stirs up dust in the gravel patch. I watch as people's bags are loaded and passengers climb aboard with a superior smile that seems to say, *You poor suckers.* I imagine they'll be settling into their air-conditioned rooms sipping Arnold Palmers while I'll be sweating miles back, toting a pack half my height like a bumbling turtle.

Pulling out gear, I throw it haphazardly into the pack. *Sleeping bag, tent, stove, cooking utensils, propane, first aid kit, clothes, food.* Miraculously, it all fits, but the bag is bursting at the seams. Testing the weight, I hoist it on my back. *Oh my God.* My knees buckle. There is no way I can carry this thing ten miles; I can't carry it fifty feet. A visual of Cheryl Strayed in *Wild* on her hands and knees trying to lift her pack—aptly nicknamed Monster—the very first time before hiking the Pacific Crest Trail comes to mind. *Beast. Demon. Bastard.* Now I get it.

Daunted, each item comes out to be scrutinized. The extra propane canister, spare food, and surplus layers get ixnayed. Every ounce of weight matters. Still, since I'm alone, there are too many items I can't do without. Running my hand across my forehead with anxiety, I feel a twinge of pressure. The lodge requires campers to check in by 2:00 p.m. to secure their reservation.

Repacking and shouldering the hefty horror, I adjust the straps. The weight is brutal, but manageable. I try not to think about the miles ahead (eight to the lodge, then two more to the campground). Setting my gaze, I lurch forward, placing one foot in front of the other.

The first few miles of the trail cut down the cliff with sharp, steep switchbacks eventually winding to the valley floor. After this comes a level, relatively easy stroll to the village—at least, this is what I tell myself. Grinding downward, the pack settles on my shoulders and I quickly start to sweat through my cotton T-shirt. The sun shines in full force, the air dry as bone. The landscape is rocky and barren with small shrubs dotting the riverbed below. I move over intermittently for the pack horses laden with gear. When I make it to the bottom of the switchbacks, I find my stride. I'm making good time and should have no problem getting to the village before 2:00 p.m. to check in. *Check in . . . My reservation . . .* I pause mid-stride. *I need my wallet to check in and pay. My wallet . . . my wallet . . . WHERE THE FUCK IS MY WALLET?*

"SHIT!" I yell, disturbing only lizards.

I know exactly where my stupid wallet is. It's locked in my car. Precisely two miles back up the cliff—the steepest, most difficult part of this entire hike.

I groan out loud. *I can't believe I've done this.*

Calculating how long it will take me to get back to the car, I know I can't carry my pack. I'll have to hide it and come back for it. The thought gives me pause. I have my expensive DSLR camera tucked on top with everything else needed to survive the next few days. Kicking myself for the careless mistake, I ditch my bag under some shrubs where I hope it will be safe.

Turning around, the trail agonizes me with vertical cutbacks all the way to the parking lot. Without the added weight, I hike fast, but don't bring water. *Rookie mistake number two.* Parched and overheated, I stumble over the final ridge. After unlocking the car, I use my newly acquired wallet to purchase a bottle of Aquafina from a Native woman with long gray braids and wrinkled chestnut skin. She's set up at a table with a cooler of drinks beside her. The ice looks so tantalizing, I wonder how much she'd charge to dump it over my head.

"You're not hiking alone, are you?" she asks.

"I am..."

Her eyes appraise mine with concern. "You need to be careful," she says, then adds, "A mountain lion was recently spotted right off the trail." *Ugh. Again?!* I think about asking her for a pen. Instead, I nod and thank her. But her warning felt more ominous, more cautionary than just a tip about a mountain lion. I shake off apprehension, turn my sweaty self around and descend a very familiar trail.

I check my watch. I'll be cutting it *really close*. I decide to jog to quicken my pace, just a light jaunt on the downhill. My heels immediately protest. Blisters appear, then burst. After chafing painfully, crimson splotches bleed through my socks. *Walking it is.*

I pass horses laden with gear, their hooves clomping noisily. One of the handlers gives me a leering smile. I keep my eyes averted, pretending not to notice. He nudges his companion. A catcall follows. Within seconds, all the handlers' eyeballs are following my every step. I ignore the men but acknowledge my naked vulnerability. *Is that what the old woman had meant?*

When I make it to my backpack, I sigh with relief. It sits untouched, waiting for me dutifully. I position my pepper spray in the outside pocket for easy access, pick it up with gratitude, and hike in earnest.

Since setting out, I've been significantly more terrified of the threats people around me pose than any animal or obstacle. The catcalls, the lingering gazes, the creepy questions. My mind races: *Can I trust them? Are there other people around? What can I use to protect myself?* These thoughts accompany me far too often when out in the wild. Sleeping alone at night in my tent, I feel exposed. Overcoming fears to drift off is a nightly routine. The sinister what-ifs have never held me back, but I resent that my safety is always, *always* the primary thing on my mind when traveling alone as a woman.

Painful miles and long hours later, I reach the small village. Clocking in at 1:55 p.m. with some satisfaction, but mostly just fatigue, I stumble into the reservation office.

"Made it!" I exclaim to the old man working the desk.

"Made what?" He looks at me quizzically.

"The two p.m. deadline to check in!"

I'm about to launch into my little debacle when he says nonchalantly, "Oh, we don't really care what time you get here, just as long as you have a reservation and you can pay in full."

I blink slowly. Digesting. Deflating. I kind of want to cry.

But I don't. I remind myself of the blue paradise that awaits. I hand over my credit card—the one I'm bleeding for—and he goes through the rules and regulations with me. He sticks the permit on my pack and points me out the door: *Just two more miles.*

They are the hardest two miles of my life. The gravel turns to sand. My boots slide around, losing all traction as I stumble along. What should have been two feels like another ten. I become desperate to be done. *This is so stupid. What was I thinking?* With every step, I will myself forward. My heels are devastated, legs unsteady. I forget about the noble cause of proving my strength and independence. I want to give up. To say screw this and check into an all-inclusive resort with a spa. *How the hell did Cheryl do it? This is only ten miles—ten!* If there was an easy pass I would take it. But there isn't. I don't have a choice.

I can't hike back out, a helicopter is unquestionably out of budget, and the lodge is completely booked. I blubber like a baby, putting one ravaged foot in front of the next, soldiering on. *Why am I even doing this?* It strikes me that perhaps all I'm subjecting myself to—bleeding, sweating, pushing these limits—do I think I deserve to be punished? Is this my penance for leaving a deeply hurting boy behind? Or is it really about being a strong, independent woman who doesn't need a man? Surely, there are easier ways.

After what feels like an eon ... salvation. Mercifully, the deep sand turns to solid rock. I find my footing and reach the final ledge. The roaring of a waterfall meets my ears. Then I see it. I stop, mesmerized. It's even more beautiful than I expected. Below me sits paradise. A lush green oasis with alluring turquoise pools surrounded by rich, red, desert sandstone. *I made it.* I make my way to the campground, pitch my tent, gingerly strip off my boots, and jump into the freezing river.

As I'm toweling off, a group of young campers wander onto the beach. One of their crew, a boy who doesn't look a day over eighteen, pulls his girlfriend by the hand toward the falls. Abruptly, he turns and kneels. *Uh-oh.* With a smile, he pulls a ring out of his khakis pocket and pops the question. *Damn.* The girl gasps in shock. With a dramatic *YES!* the ring is slid on her finger. Their friends snap photos as I awkwardly shimmy my wet body out of the background.

They are so young, just babies! I want to ask: *Are you sure you know what you're doing?* I force a smile and offer my congratulations. Inwardly my heart aches almost as bad as my feet, almost as painful as the realization that was also me—just a baby—who thought she knew what she was doing.

I return to camp where a family of five have pitched their tents near mine.

"So . . . what are you doing out here all alone?" the father asks.

"Trying to start over after a divorce," I admit, still raw from my engagement photobomb.

Their son, a little younger than me, asks, "Did you marry for love, money, or a visa?" His parents shoot him a sharp look. I take my time.

"Love," I say simply, although nothing about it is simple at all.

Later that evening, I walk back to the falls where a thunderous roar reverberates through the canyon walls. Prepping my DSLR, I wait for the moonrise. The darkness greets my vulnerable heart like an old friend as reminders of my own proposal crash around her fortifications.

I find a seat as the stars shine down and a luminous glow grows brighter and brighter toward the top of the ridge. Slowly, the moon appears—almost full but not quite, swollen and luminescent. Its reflection sparkles in the water as it falls from the burnt-orange cliffs. The universe dances in refracted light that dazzles. The entire cosmos is on display in the rainbow colors of the mist. I stand up in awe, neglecting my camera altogether. I forget about my hurting heart and blistered feet. I lose myself in wonder gazing up at the perfection before me.

Standing entranced, I witness what I long to be. The illuminated cascade is wild and unapologetic, striking and powerful. She has been made fiercer after enduring the desert. She stubbornly refuses to be contained, a mass of force that belongs to no one but herself. She's unique and totally her own, leaving all who witness her breathless. She offers me something to live by.

Droplets of cool mist form on my skin, glowing like pearls in the moonlight. Whatever it takes to be like her. Wherever this all leads. I've wandered through the desert already. I'm not punishing myself; I'm prevailing. If the pain and trials along the way result in something so magnificent and wholly beautiful, I choose to wander the same trail again and again. Every choice that led to the here and now . . . it was all so, so worth it.

21

A SAFE PLACE

I arrive back to California in the fading twilight. Although it's been a few years since I moved away, when I pass through the state border, I breathe deep. It feels like home. I pull up to the marina as the first evening stars twinkle above my new residence: the thirty-six-foot sailboat my parents live on. My new roommates, Mom and Dad, are in the parking lot waiting with open arms.

My parents are high school sweethearts. They've been together since Mom was fifteen and Dad was sixteen. She sat behind him in math class and stared, lovesick, at the back of his head. When he wanted to ask her out, he didn't have her phone number, so he called every matching surname in the local town's phonebook until he reached her. On their picnics at the Laguna Beach cliffs, Dad would strum his guitar, singing Bob Dylan songs. He bought his first boat and named it after her. When my dad proposed at nineteen, they kept their engagement a secret for weeks. There was no big surprise, no glittering ring, they just sat side by side on a river when it dawned on them: *Why not get married? Should we do it? Let's just do it.* They still make big decisions this exact same, impulsive way. My mom wore her mother's wedding dress. For their honeymoon, they took their Volkswagen Bus up the California coast.

Their first home was a sailboat in Newport Beach. Dad had a mustache and long flowing hair. Mom wore ribbons and made her own dresses. She went to nursing school while Dad sold boats. One of her favorite scents in the world was when he would come home smelling like teak and resin. Six years after "I do," they had their first baby. They started a family and didn't stop until they had eight children. They grew up together in every way, experiencing every major life transition, choosing to remain side by side, even when it had seemed impossible.

After becoming empty nesters, they sold everything and moved from our little town in the Sierras onto their 1978 sailboat back in Newport Beach, not far from where they'd lived as newlyweds. Retiring on the boat has been their dream. The happiest I've ever seen my parents is on the water.

A Nautica ballcap is pulled low over Dad's semi-bald head, a smattering of gray hair protruding from the sides. He's wearing beige shorts and flip-flops; a bright aqua button-up stretches across his portly belly. He smiles, his hawkish nose crinkling. Mom wears a matching aqua dress and smile.

"Welcome home, Sarah May," she sings. "We're so happy to have you stay for as long as you need!"

"Ahoy, maties," I call, hugging them tightly.

The three of us walk down to their slip. As I step from solid land onto the dock, it sways from side to side, buffeted by the outgoing tide. Their boat is nestled between someone's expensive toys, a two-story powerboat and another gleaming monohull. We step into the cockpit, and a hatch slides open to reveal the living space below. To the left, a small galley and dining area. To the right, a navigation station and sofa. A hand-carved door leads to the middle cabin—their bedroom—containing a full-size bed and two small closets. Then, at the bow, a compact, V-shaped bathroom hosts a toilet and handheld shower.

They've graciously made space for me on their floating home: two small cupboards to keep my clothes in and the sofa to crash on. The rest of my belongings, the big boxes I shipped back from the East Coast, sit in a storage unit nearby. The plan is to stay with them until I get back on my feet and figure out what comes next.

It's a classic millennial cliché, moving back in with mom and dad. For some it's due to crippling student loan debt, for others the inability to find a decent-paying job. But whatever the cause of return, it's usually *not* onto a sailboat. After moving across the country for graduate school, marriage, and a career (aka the societal equivalent of having my life together), it's humbling. It's been six years since I lived under their roof. Now, I squeeze in under their mast, trading my hiking boots for sea legs. *Anchors away to my ego.* But as I drop my bag onto the sofa, I'm also aware what a blessing it is that I have a place to retreat to, that I have parents who welcome me with open arms.

When night falls, I nestle into a sleeping bag. Not five feet from me, on the other side of a thin wood door, their loud snores reverberate in my ears. I jam in earplugs, but it's like a foghorn in the quiet harbor. I lie awake, thinking about the last few hours of my road trip.

Earlier that day, somewhere on a stretch of the Mojave, Nick had called. We hadn't spoken since Florida; I'd been avoiding it. Unsure of what to say, I was apprehensive when his name popped up. I was ending my trip on such a good note, in such a positive place. Still, I pulled off the highway and answered the call. Feeling responsible, the burden of his well-being resting unnecessarily in my psyche. I looked out at the desert landscape as we made small talk. A tumbleweed bounced lazily across the road. In a veiled tone, he asked if I'd met anyone. I knew what he meant. When I didn't give him a straight answer, he pressed again.

"I'm not going to talk about this with you," I said.

"What's the difference? We're not together anymore, so it doesn't matter, right?" He pushed and pushed until some defense within, where I knew I had no obligation to tell him anything, fell away.

"Yes . . . I met lots of people."

"And did you *get* with anyone?"

After a minute of strained silence, I conceded. "I did."

I felt his anger before I heard it. "How many?" he demanded.

"Two," I said eventually.

He gave a mocking laugh. "Well, good for you. I guess we're even now."

I sat stunned. I shouldn't have told him. I knew what was at stake. "It's not the same thing," I said quietly.

It didn't matter. He felt justified, like now he had something over me.

"You know," he said haughtily, "I deserve their thanks for all I taught you in bed."

I recoiled. I hated myself for playing into this. "Nick, stop it. That's enough."

But it wasn't. We continued with a back-and-forth that got us nowhere. When I hung up, I was filled with regret for answering in the first place. It felt like I'd been punched in the gut. I was the addict who couldn't say no, struggling to detach from her drug of choice.

All the energy and enthusiasm I had, the high of coming off my trip, was sucked right out of me. It's a slow unlearning, remaking myself apart from the role I once played. It was my fault for answering the call, for giving my power away. This fault of mine carried me all the way across the desert to my new home and into my sleeping bag where it keeps me company still, wide awake, until nothingness consumes me at last.

My parents and I settle into a new routine as roommates. When they aren't traveling, we drive up to Peet's Coffee to sit outside by a fountain, each of us journaling. They first modeled the practice to me when I was in my teens, and it had become a daily ritual. I run around Balboa Island or up on the cliffs overlooking the harbor where the coastal fog burns off into sunshine bliss. In the evenings, we play cards or pile into their bed to watch cheesy rom-coms. We go out to happy hours or cook comfort food, eating on the boat's deck as the sun sets over the marina. Mom surprises me with cupcakes from Sprinkles and fills my storage locker with Vitamin Waters for my hot yoga obsession. I get a waitressing job at an upscale pizza place up the street.

For so long I couldn't imagine being happy again, feeling normal again, not thinking about Nick incessantly. I couldn't fathom moving on as if the earth underneath my feet hadn't given way. But every day it becomes easier. The sun sets. The stars come out. I sleep. Coffee tastes just as amazing every single morning. I eat. My body carries me to different places. My smile reaches up to my eyes. When I laugh it feels like being twice-born. Life happens. And I am here, doing okay, sometimes even good. These tiny miracles.

I realize that living with my parents on the boat is the most time we've ever spent just the three of us. Growing up with seven siblings, as a middle child, at times I felt overlooked, lost in the chaos. Especially since my parents were finding their way through their own reckoning, both personally and in their marriage. Now, they're emotionally available. They show up in a way they could not when I was a child. Intuitively, I know this time is a much-needed gift after all I've been through. It feels as if I've lived a lifetime of pain in just six months. I need help remembering who I was before all this.

Ever so slowly, I talk to them about Nick. I arrive at a place where talking is cathartic and they're able to give me exactly what I need: a safe space.

Bessel van der Kolk writes in his best-selling book, *The Body Keeps the Score*, that: "Traumatized human beings recover in the context of relationships: The role of those relationships is to provide physical and emotional safety, including safety from feeling shamed, admonished, or judged, and to bolster the courage to tolerate, face, and process the reality of what has happened." Kolk continues, "The critical issue is reciprocity: being truly heard and seen by the people around us, feeling that we are held in someone else's mind and heart. For our physiology to calm down, heal, and grow we need a visceral feeling of safety. No doctor can write a prescription for friendship and love."[3]

While I don't yet know to call what I carry trauma, I do know that my parents and friends (my people) are my prescription. If not for the loving, supportive relationships I have with friends and family, I wouldn't have made it through the darkness. When I broke so magnificently, it was hard to remember what I was living for. People reminded me.

People like Max and Trina, who took me in, providing unconditional support and a place to stay. Like Cat and Daryn, who showed up at the hospital, donated their vacation hours, and accepted my decision to leave with grace. Like Lori and her family, who embraced me as their own. Like my best friend, who answered a desperate call at 3:00 a.m. Like the Troops, who helped me remember to laugh and play. Like Aaron, who organized a thoughtful girls' night out for me in New Orleans. Like Mom and Dad, who are re-nurturing me in their loving presence, where it's safe to break, and they simply break with me.

People catch me as I fall, giving me the safety net I need to not disappear completely. They remind me of the light in the depths of despair. They tell me it will be okay when I don't believe it. They point me home when I'm lost, back to the daughter, sister, and friend they know and love. There are no requests to change who I am or where I am, messiness and all. There is no judgment about my decisions, no one saying *I told you so*, no timeline on when I should have my shit together. They teach me that it's okay to ask for help, to break, to receive. This is belonging. And belonging is saving me.

I find safety in the waiting arms of these beautiful people who hold me in their hearts and minds. Being re-nurtured provides the gentle, safe place where I can heal. I utter a prayer of gratitude for the people who love me when I do not yet know how to love myself fully.

May we all have these people, cherish them, and keep them close. Perhaps one day, we can retain hope for another when their spark is dim; our arms and hearts can hold all their pieces until they are ready to rise from the ashes.

22

GOODBYES

I sit at the end of the dock, watching the sun set over the boats in Newport Beach. My bare feet dangle toward the water. The colors that streak across the last of the sky are reflected below: mesmerizing hues of smoky orange and lilac lavender. They give way to a dusky indigo smattered with stars' first shining.

Nick asked to talk again, but I stalled. He wanted to send flowers, but I refused. Part of me knew this conversation was coming, that this was inevitable. Somehow, I'm still unprepared. Whether wrong or right, I withheld having this conversation because he seemed so fragile. He still does. He's hoping for a miracle; I'm ready for closure. Before I even left, the death of our relationship had been cemented. While I was watching it dry, laying it to rest, he was holding out hope that the grave was made of sand, that what we buried could be resurrected. I was long gone and he was standing in the exact same place.

On the call, Nick reads from a letter that he says he wrote especially for this conversation and will later send to me. His voice wavers.

"Sarah, I'm sorry. I'm sorry for everything I put you through, for taking you for granted, for breaking the promises I made. If I could take back all the destruction I've caused, I would. I know what I've done can never be righted and I know it would take a long time to forgive, but through it all I've had the realization . . . I want you.

"I want you by my side for the rest of my life. It won't be easy, but the best things in life are worth fighting for. I don't want to look back and say I wish I would have tried harder. Until that day comes when you tell me to stop, I won't give up on us. You're worth it and always have been . . .

"Please, give the man you know I'm capable of being one more chance. You're not fighting this alone anymore if you still want to fight. It's us against the world if you want it to be. I don't want to end like this. I love you, Sarah."

Silence fills the phone line as he waits for my response. His words echo in my head. Not so long ago, I would have done anything to hear this speech. But the pleas arrive when it's too late.

Why is it that we take for granted what we have when we have it and it's only when we lose it that it becomes clear how precious it truly was? I have finally begun to value myself enough to know what I deserve. I didn't for too long and that still makes me sad, but now I find my voice. My courage. It's time. Time to tell him what I've known in my heart for months. To speak what I thought was clear when we signed a separation agreement, when I packed up my life and set out on the road. There is no going back.

I utter the words he doesn't want to hear. "It's over, Nick. I can't do this anymore. We're done."

His voice cracks. "You fought so hard for me. You held on for so long, I thought . . . I thought you wouldn't give up. We promised, forever and a day. We can still have that—we can still get it back, Sarah."

"That promise was broken," I remind him. "I gave it all I had, and it wasn't enough—"

He interjects, "It is . . . It was . . . I just got lost. I was weak. I'm so sorry. But I'm finally finding myself again. I thought you would be waiting for me. If you can find it in your heart to forgive me, I'll spend the rest of my life proving it to you."

My voice falters. The gravity of the words are heavy off my tongue. "I can't, Nick. It's too late. It was all too much."

He cries harder, his sobs filling the space between us. "Please," he whispers. "You're just scared of getting hurt again. Give me another chance."

My heart aches, my strength diminishes, and suddenly all I feel is exhaustion. An acute, soul-sucking depletion that consumes the life force from my very bones. I know this feeling. I lived this feeling. I close my eyes. If I choose him, the rest of my life would be this feeling.

"I'm sorry," I say. And I am.

I'm sorry we're here, that our story ended like this. Sorry for the dreams we lost and the death of the life we imagined together. The greatness of my grief was the measure of my love. I'd descended to the depths to try and save us. Now, it's about saving myself. More than I'm sorry, I'm sure. This is it. It has to be. There will be no more opportunities for further harm or heartbreak. There is no way to ever trust him or myself with him. There is no future for us.

When I hang up, the sky has grown dark. A cold breeze sends goose bumps across my arms as I shiver at the edge of the dock. I'm worried about him, about what he could do, his mental state. I no longer love him, but I still care deeply. *Will I ever stop worrying? Will this guilt ever go away?* I pick myself up and crawl into my sleeping bag on the boat. Exhausted, I turn on my side, and in the silence of the harbor, with the gentle rocking of the waves, I cry myself to sleep. And then . . . my parents' snores startle me awake.

When Nick and I were newlyweds, we had so little money that we couldn't afford furniture for our first apartment. We had 1,000 square feet of studio space filled with nothing but our suitcases and a mattress on the floor. The apartment itself was out of our budget. We lived paycheck to paycheck. With the little cash we received from the wedding, we decided to buy furniture.

I walked into an antique store one day when I saw it—an old, weathered black credenza. I ran my hand over the smooth wood. I loved it. I couldn't explain why, but I wanted it more than anything. It would have no useful function in our bare space. I should've been looking at bed frames or a kitchen table so we wouldn't have to eat dinner on the floor every night. I left the store telling myself it was silly, but I couldn't stop thinking about it. I waited a few days and told myself that if it was still there when I went back then it was meant to be, I would buy it.

I returned eagerly. There it was. I loaded it all alone into the back of my car. I wanted to surprise Nick when he came home from work. I situated it against the studio wall so when we walked in, it would be the first thing we'd see. I put our newly framed wedding photos and big white pillar candles on it. I stepped back and sighed. It was perfect. But when Nick came home, he was less than pleased I had decided to spend some of our precious wedding money on something so useless. He didn't fight me, but he didn't like it either. I didn't care. Every time I looked at it, it made me happy. Strange what a small thing with seemingly no purpose can do. That credenza was the first thing to come and the very last thing to go.

When I sold our furniture and packed up my life, I couldn't bring myself to get rid of it. I also couldn't bring it to California, so I left it with Nick. Inside we'd kept our mementos: all the letters we had written each other, love notes, photos, ticket stubs, dried flowers he'd given me, even the Forever Rose (*the world's longest-lasting luxury rose, a real blossom preserved in twenty-four-karat gold!*). All the small things we collected along the way that eventually meant nothing.

I fly back to the East Coast six months after I left that life behind, returning to wrap up the divorce. Only a month or so after that final phone call with Nick, I'm ready to have my maiden name back, to put our marriage behind me. We still have the damn credenza. Filled with reminders of our relationship, it's become a visceral reminder, something once dearly loved that now just takes up space.

༄

I arrange to pick it up from Nick and gift it to Max and Trina. Looking back, I wonder: *Why didn't I just ask them to get it? Why did I agree to see him? Was there a small part of me that wanted to?*

I borrow Max's car and pull up outside Nick's house. My heart beats fast. *Be calm, be calm, be calm*, I coach myself. I'd told Nick he could leave it outside, but he insisted on helping me load it. He sits on the porch steps, wearing gym shorts and a tank-top, a pitiful look on his face. We load it, then stand awkwardly.

"You look good," he says.

I look down at my purple blouse and black shorts. "Thanks," I say.

His voice cracks, tears well in his eyes when he speaks next. "I'm so sorry, Sarah. I'm sorry for everything."

For what it's worth, I believe him. He appears genuine. When I speak, he actually seems to hear my words, looking at me instead of through me. It's like he's slowly coming back online after being dead inside. For half an hour we stand talking in the crisp fall air. He shows me his new tattoo. I'd paid the deposit for an appointment as an anniversary gift before I left. At the time, he didn't seem to care. He tries to reminisce about the past, to tell me it wasn't all bad, that he hopes I'll remember the good. But I can't go back there with him. I'm looking ahead at a future that's already so much brighter.

"Are you happy?" he asks.

"I am," I say truthfully, "I hope one day you can be too."

"I'm getting there..." he says.

I stand frozen, unsure of what comes next. He wraps me up in a hug. Leaning in, he kisses the top of my head and whispers, "Goodbye, Sarah May."

Stepping away, I'm ready to be done. I get into Max's car and back out of the driveway as Nick watches me pull away. I roll down the windows and let the warm air filter in as dappled sunlight falls across the road. I realize my hands are shaking as I grip the steering wheel. This time, I'm the one who doesn't look back. This is the last time I will ever see the man who had been my husband.

Max and Trina help me unload the credenza. I go through the drawers, pulling out all our old letters, photos, and keepsakes. The Forever Rose finally gets trashed. I run my hand lovingly along the weathered wood. Strange how such a small thing with seemingly no purpose had held so much. I keep the letters and throw everything else into the garbage. I want them for the story that one day, I'll be ready to tell.

23

RESPONSIBILITY

I sit with twenty other students enrolled in a yoga teacher training. We're gathered in San Diego to receive a 200-hour certification that will allow us to audition as instructors. When I discovered the power of yoga, bawling my eyes out in a steamy room with strangers, I knew I wanted to dive deeper. Today is one of the last days of our spiritual training program, and over the course of the intensives, I've been immersed in a foreign world.

During the past few weeks we've memorized asanas (yoga positions); led each other through sequences; spent a day in meditative silence; stepped onto the mat blindfolded; cried, laughed, and grown together. Among the eclectic mix is Blaze, the tattooed man in his mid-thirties who always looks like he's dressed for Burning Man and who taught us how to om properly. Tori, a new mom, who never wears deodorant or shaves and touts drinking her own breast milk. Cielo, who eats mostly kale and claims she can see auras. There's Jan, a young military wife I can relate with. Then there is me, a recent divorcée raised conservative Christian, wide-eyed about all of it.

Our teachers have covered yoga basics, sequencing, anatomy, and adjustments. They also dove deep into the spiritual aspects of the training: reincarnation, angels, dreams, spirits, energy, chakras, astrology, and more. I'm not sure what to think about their advice for putting salt in the corners of a room to clear the bad vibes, their warnings about EMFs, or if crystals actually have any special powers. But I've come to adore my cohort—smells, sorcery, superstitions, and all.

Lotus flowers are splashed across the walls of the training room. Flo, our fairy-like teacher, with short gray hair and adorned in long, flowing shawls, instructs us to set up cushions and divides us into groups of five.

"One person will lie on the cushion, and the others will spread around their feet, arms, and head," she directs. "When I play the music, use your hands to channel love and light into the person lying down. When you hear the music switch, I want you to wrap them up, holding them tenderly in a safe embrace."

I have no idea what she means, but the past few weeks have been an exercise in discomfort, so the instructions hardly phase me. Luckily, Cielo is in my group—the girl who sees auras. I assume she knows what she's doing, so I follow her lead.

The music plays and those of us stationed around the person on the cushion sweep our hands inches above their body. I watch Cielo. Her eyes are closed and she seems focused. I imagine my hands have magical abilities, that somehow with each sweep over the body, an invisible force flows from my palms. We keep moving our hands and when the music switches, *hallelujah – hallelujah – hallelujah*, we embrace the person on the cushion, wrapping them up in a group hug. One by one, as if on cue, each person breaks down when we hug them, sobbing into our arms. We're instructed not to say anything, so we just keep holding them.

Eventually, it's my turn. I self-consciously arrange myself as everyone settles around me. Our group is made up of all women except

Burning Man Blaze, sitting to my left, next to my heart. I close my eyes and take a deep breath, trying to relax.

When the music plays, even though my eyes are closed, I can sense the hands hovering above me. I become acutely aware of Blaze with his masculine energy. All I can focus on is his presence. When the music peaks, something shifts abruptly. *He no longer feels like Blaze.* There is a sharp change. I realize, startled, *I feel Nick.* His presence takes over. It's unmistakable. The way Nick would carry himself, the way he'd take up space. I can even smell him. I'm overcome. Not with anger. Not with sadness. With *softness.* Somehow, here in the studio, three thousand miles away from where I know Nick to actually be, I also know without a doubt that some part of him is here with me. As this ghost sits next to me, his hands over my heart, tears form.

In this space of something occurring that should be impossible, I have a vision. My green eyes meet his brown ones, our gaze locked, lost in each other, just like at our wedding. Words come to my lips from somewhere beyond myself, somewhere inexplicable. *I'm sorry,* I say. *I'm so, so sorry.* My body shakes violently as the hands hover above me. In a different world, I hear the music change. *Hallelujah – hallelujah – hallelujah.* Suddenly arms are lifting me up, wrapping around me, holding me tight. I give in, surrendering, feeling Nick's arms hold me in a loving embrace.

When the music subsides and I wipe my face with my sleeve, I know what transpired doesn't make any logical sense. I also know it was as real as the cushions underneath me. I look at Burning Man Blaze. "Thank you," I whisper. "You don't know what you just did for me."

"I was supposed to let it happen for you," he responds vaguely. I never ask him what he means because I don't need to. For me, it's only confirmation that something supernatural has occurred.

What happened was between Nick's soul and my soul. At first, I questioned why. *Why was I the one apologizing?* It would have been the easier choice to remain a victim in the confines of anger and blame, proclaiming, *I didn't deserve what happened. Nick cheated and lied. He broke our marriage.* It's not that Nick is no longer accountable for his behavior; he will always be. *But so am I.* One of the hardest and most terrifying places I can go is the place where suffering meets responsibility. Healing means taking an honest look at the role I played. What Nick had done spoke to his wounds, but maybe what I had tolerated somehow spoke to mine. I finally ask: *In what ways might I have chosen a path that led to so much suffering?*

In our marriage, I'd often been blind to my own faults. I think about the times Nick said, "You're always right, I'm always wrong." *Was there some truth in that?* When he cheated, I recall how my anger and heartbreak were also buoyed by righteousness. I felt justified when I tried to protect Nick from abusing himself, but it seemed I was incapable of protecting myself when he chose to abuse me. My emotional immaturity and jealousy only added fuel to the raging fire of his insecurities—a fire I could never quench. And when I found out about the first affair, clutching a gun in my hand, sobbing hysterically, was there some part of me that wanted him to rescue me like I believed I had rescued him? Was I desperate for him to show me he loved me as much as I loved him? As I reflect on those moments, I realize that apologizing *to him* is how I take responsibility for *my part* in the dynamic *we* created.

Ownership is a critical part of the process. Reconciling within by taking full responsibility for how I went about getting my needs met, what I played into, created, and excused. And while it's true that I didn't deserve what happened to me, being wounded is never about deservingness.

Dr. Edith Eger, Holocaust survivor and author of *The Gift*, writes: "We can be wounded and accountable. Responsible and innocent . . . We don't get to choose what happens to us, but we do get to choose how we respond to our experience. . . . We're called to be accountable . . . to take responsibility even in situations we didn't cause or choose."[4]

I have every right to my pain, but what I do with it will determine the rest of my life and the story I'll tell. Stories have immense power. They shape the narrative of a life. Forever telling the story of being a victim siphons away power from personal responsibility and accountability. *Why did I choose who I chose? What did that choice say about me? Why was I so complacent with the dysfunction?*

In the vision, as I looked into Nick's eyes, I saw sadness. His brown eyes brimmed with the pain of hurting someone he cared for. *What if all along, Nick was a mirror, reflecting back to me all the hurting places, all the unmet needs, all that longed for reclamation, within myself?* In this holy instant, I understand that he offered me all he could. I'm left with the learning.

Later that night, after my parents have gone to sleep, I write a letter to Nick. Penned for my own benefit, never to be sent.

> *I knew you were there. You're so familiar to me. I know the energy around you, the presence you bring when you walk into a room. I knew in that moment with my heart beating wildly, tears streaming down my face, pain leaving my chest like sheets of metal being lifted off, that you were helping me set myself free.*
>
> *You may not understand now, but I hope one day you know what it feels like—the sweetest taste of surrender, the truest form of release. I said that I didn't love you, but I realized in*

that moment that I do. I will always love your soul, even if I fell out of love with the man. Every soul deserves to be loved because every soul is love.

I've been through the darkness, and some days the haze plagues me still. The hardest part about it all is learning to love myself. I'm learning that love is gentle, that it begins and ends only within. I've learned that it's easy to be selfish when you've been hurt, but that asking for forgiveness and extending it are the only ways forward. I've learned that no matter what each of us goes through, we always have a choice of who we choose to be, how we pick up the pieces, how we become.

I had a dream about you the other night. Things were just like before I left. I was fighting so hard . . . trying to convince you of our love, but you couldn't be convinced. I woke up to the sun shining, the ocean's salt on my lips, the gentle rocking of the waves, and I felt safer than I have in a long time. I'll never question if I could have done anything more; I'll never look back with regret. Your soul was so heavy, and it was never mine to carry. We both know it was my time to go.

This has given me a second chance. Maybe you were meant to teach me, and me you. I only hope it gifts you as much as it has gifted me. I hope you find your path to freedom, as I'm finding mine. I hope one day, when I fall in love with someone else, you can be happy for me as I will be happy for you. I hope you go on adventures and have a family and do all the things we always talked about doing. I hope you can understand when I go about the world and write my stories and have my heart expanded by all I ever wanted.

Life is a big, beautiful mess and I wouldn't trade it for the world. These past months I have begun to come home to *myself. I've felt the heat rise up in my bones, the desire for life. I've felt a full spectrum of everything under the sun, and to me, the world is only more lovely. The soul is a resilient, beautiful thing. I hope you can learn to embrace the light of all you are, and perhaps one day, I can know we both learned how to be free.*

24

BAND-AID

On the final night of yoga teacher training, I go out to celebrate with girlfriends from the program. Someone buys us a bottle of champagne, and we dance at a dive bar until last call. As the night dwindles, we sway down the street. Hippies play guitar, passing around joints and drinking from brown paper bags. Girls in high heels teeter past. All night my friends had tried to pair me with eligible bachelors. No luck . . . until now.

"Sarah," says one of my friends, "look how cute he is."

I look up to lock eyes with a man sitting in the passenger seat of a nearby parked Uber. He's distinctly handsome, mid-twenties, with curly hair bleached blond from the sun, tanned skin, and penetrating eyes. For a moment, we just stare. Suddenly, he smiles. Raising a hand, he beckons me over. I feel magnetically drawn to him, pulled into his orbit. He seems familiar, a kind of recognition passes between us, but I'm certain we've never met. I traipse over to the parked car.

He rolls down the window. "Hey," he says. "Where you girls headed?"

I hear my girlfriends excitedly whispering behind me. Casually, I respond, "We're not sure . . ."

"You should come with us. We're headed to a party . . . jump in." He motions to another man in the back seat. "I'm Sam by the way." He flashes another smile.

"Sarah." I smile back, sizing him up from outside the car. He's short, but athletic. A black T-shirt accentuates his muscles; dark jeans hug his hips. I turn and consult the girls. They don't hesitate. We pile into the Uber and head to an unknown destination.

The party is at his friend's—the man in the back seat—and it's really just a party of us. I don't mind; I'm so intrigued by Sam that the setting doesn't matter. When the bag of ecstasy comes out, everyone else partakes. Sam looks at me questioningly. I've dabbled with weed, but never anything harder.

My girlfriends assure me, "If you want to try it, we've got your back."

I consider, curious. Impulsively, I grab a pill, place it on my tongue, and swallow. *No great night ever started with eating a salad, right?*

An hour later, I still don't feel anything. Everyone else is rolling like they're at a rave. "Take more!" they urge. So I do. We dissolve another pill in a glass of water and I gulp it down. Another half hour passes. Still nothing. "Maybe it doesn't affect you? Try one more time." So I do. *Strike three.*

Minutes later, it hits. Hard.

The sensations in my body are so overwhelming that just breathing requires conscious effort. *Inhale now? Yes, breathe. Okay, release. You know how to do this*, I tell myself. Everyone is so loud. Actually, *everything* is loud. An onslaught of sound that somehow has color. I can't stop clenching my damn jaw. I sit on the couch, gripping the cushion like a lifeline. Waves of color blur my vision, and my entire body seems to vibrate.

Sam notices my pale face. He sits beside me and places his hand on my back.

"Are you okay?" he asks.

I think I tell him no. Can we undo this? I took too much. Why are the walls pulsating? Why does his touch feel so good?

"C'mon, let's go outside," he says, taking my hand and leading me onto the balcony.

As soon as we step outside, the fresh air offers instant relief. I sit on a barstool, taking deep breaths. *Inhale now? Yes, breathe. Okay, release.* Sam coaxes me through the peaks, distracting me with conversation. When the worst of it passes, we become lost in words. We have so much in common. Meeting tonight feels like serendipity. We're discovering something wonderful. He likes me. I like him. He is being so sweet, so kind. He seems so good, like such a caring person. Hours pass like that, or is it minutes?

"*Where* did you come from?" he asks with wonder, as if I fell out of the sky.

It's a long story, I think. But before I have a chance to respond, he's putting his arms around me, pulling me toward him. We are kissing. Kissing feels like how I thought the ecstasy would. Like standing in a fucking rainbow.

The next morning, everyone is spread about the living room, hungover, coming down. Sam sits on the floor; my head rests in his lap. Absentmindedly, he strokes my hair. Already, there is a familiarity between us, a comfort. Maybe it's the ecstasy, maybe it's chemistry, but either way, I'm enamored. When everyone is roused, he orders us girls an Uber and kisses me goodbye.

When Sam calls a few days later to ask me out on a date, I can hardly contain my excitement. I haven't been able to stop thinking about him. Using the small bathroom on the boat, I curl my hair and shave my legs. I manage to apply makeup despite the gentle rocking. Gold sequin shirt, black skirt. I drive down to San Diego and we go out for a drink. Then three. We stay up all night talking, again. "I like you *so, so* much," he tells me. And just like that, I'm swept away.

I wasn't sure after everything I went through that I would love again, trust again. The fear of being hurt hangs like armor over my heart. Being vulnerable after being so betrayed is terrifying. But Sam feels different; he *is* different. I like him so much that I choose to take the risk.

I'm still not officially divorced—the decree is still pending from the separation—but marriage feels long behind me. I don't stay single very long.

Being with Sam is such a radical contrast from the heaviness with Nick. Our dynamic is playful and light. He makes me laugh. We party with friends almost every weekend and drink our way into a fast romance. Soon, I meet his family. Then, he's on the sailboat meeting Mom and Dad. A surfer, he takes me to the beach and pushes me into waves on his longboard, hollering with excitement when I stand up. We ride bikes along the coast, have picnics on the sand. On Halloween, he officially introduces me to friends as his girlfriend. There's no conversation about it. There doesn't need to be. I jump ship from my marriage and into his arms. Falling back in love is easier than I thought it would be.

When I self-consciously tell him what transpired with Nick, all he says is, "Wow . . . I feel sorry for him." I find the response strange. I can tell he doesn't understand the extent of my undoing. His world has never been destroyed. He's never had to rebuild from the ashes. At first, I don't mind. All I want is light and he meets me there. So I bury it.

Unconsciously, our relationship becomes a kind of Band-Aid. Our love covers the wound so conveniently I practically forget it's there at all. And for a long time, we're good this way, great even. Happy, carefree. But inevitably, that which is disavowed finds its way to the surface. Wounds fester. The shadows of the past never disappear; they simply linger on the periphery.

25
TRIGGERED

I get a sales job in San Diego and move off the sailboat to be closer to Sam. My roommates are sad to see me go after six months of buoyant bonding and reluctantly say goodbye. At first, I move into a Craigslist house with a single father and his high school–aged son, the only affordable option I find in North County. Mr. Craigslist's ex-girlfriend had taken all the furniture, but he said he would soon replace it. Months later, still furniture-less, he gets a puppy that cries all day while I work from home. I share a bathroom with his teenage son—terrified to touch anything in the cesspool that it is (I have six brothers, *I know things*). Mr. Craigslist brings home Tinder dates and on the other side of my wall, I can hear *everything*. Needless to say, when Sam suggests moving in together after six months of dating, I jump at the chance.

We manage to rent a small ocean view apartment. The first night, we christen it with red wine, pizza, and a slow dance in the living room. We start a life together and begin to fill it with sweet memories. I finally feel like I've landed on my feet, and the more distance I put between myself and the past, the better. Until the past barges back in.

Nick's name pops up in a text message as I'm driving to a work meeting.

Can we talk?

Momentarily blindsided, my breath catches. Silence fills the space between my ears even though the radio is on full blast. It's been over a year since we've spoken. Time in which I've moved on with my life and he has no part in it.

As my car flies up the freeway at seventy miles per hour, I'm filled with instantaneous fear just seeing his name. My heart races, my hands shake, my mouth goes dry. I feel so overwhelmed by the onslaught of emotions I want to cancel my work meeting. Everything in my body wants to escape itself. The world goes topsy-turvy as irrational thoughts skirt my brain. I think about accelerating my car to a point where I can't feel my anger. I want to scream until I lose my voice, to tell the next person on the street about the horrors I endured. I'm unglued. Weak, explosive, unstable.

I swallow my emotions, bottle the response, and take the work meeting. I tell myself I'm overreacting, while inwardly, I feel obliterated. *What's happening?* I thought I had left Nick in the past. *Hadn't I forgiven him when I had the vision during the yoga teacher training? Why do I feel so reactive?* It's as if the ground has opened up underneath me. I fall back into a time where nothing is safe, nothing can be trusted, not my new life, and especially not myself. I want to run until I disappear.

I text Nick back when the nausea fades.

What about?

My phone pings.

There's a lawsuit from the crash, some legal stuff.

That evening, I sit on the edge of the couch, alone in the apartment.

Sam has a work event and will be out all evening. When my phone rings, Nick's name on the screen, I brace myself.

"Hi, Nick."

"Sarah, hi . . . thanks for getting back to me. I really appreciate it."

The sound of his voice. So familiar. So foreign. I'm barely breathing. Sitting like a statue.

"Sure," I say. "What's up?"

"There's a lawsuit from the crash. It's been a few years in the making, but basically, because we were married at that time, they need you to sign some documents."

"So, you finally reached a settlement? You'll get a payout?"

He pauses. "Yeah . . ."

"And why do I need to sign these papers?"

"I think they need to be sure you won't sue them. But we can't proceed until they receive your signature."

The conversation is strained, awkward.

"How much do you think you'll get?" I ask.

"I'm not sure yet, maybe a hundred thousand dollars . . . but after the lawyer fees it won't be much . . . I have a lot of debt from all the surgeries. There's a medical lien . . ." He trails off.

Wouldn't the military have paid for his medical expenses?

"So, just to be clear, by signing these papers, I'm waiving my right to any compensation?"

"Technically . . . yes."

I can't stop thinking about the loan I took out for our wedding, the one I'll be paying back for years with interest while he gets a hefty settlement.

"Nick . . . I hope when you finally get the money, you'll help pay back our wedding loan."

"Any payout will be a long time," he says, "but when it's received, I promise I'll remember."

I don't promise anything back. "Send the paperwork and I'll look it over."

He sighs. "Thank you, Sarah, I really appreciate it. It would be a huge help."

Receiving the documents fills me with bitter memories and resentment. Anger that I undoubtedly will not get paid back for the loan, that he needs this from me, that he's interrupting the storyline of my life when I'm moving on. *Should I get an attorney? After all, aren't I entitled? It isn't fair that I have to pay back our wedding...*

I wrestle back and forth for weeks, unable to make up my mind. He needs one more thing and I don't want to give another inch. I've done enough. I want restitution. I consider consulting an attorney. I confide in Sam. "Whatever you think is best," he tells me. He doesn't like talking about my past, about Nick.

Almost a month passes and I still can't make up my mind. The pressure mounts; I receive calls from his attorney, more texts from Nick, even inappropriate messages from his mom. Making a decision becomes unavoidable.

What do I truly want?

To be free.

I realize that I'm playing small by being vengeful, by choosing to be engaged with him in this way. This isn't the woman I'm working hard to become. It certainly isn't the energy, attachment, or emotions that I want consuming me. Do I really want Nick back in my life, in any capacity? *No.*

As soon as I arrive at my decision, I feel peace for the first time in weeks. A lightness washes over me and I know I have to let it go. Let him go, the loan, my debt, my resentment. Moving forward there will be nothing else, no other reason to ever be in contact again. Unless by some miracle he honors his word. To some it may look like surrender, but to me it's liberation. I sign the settlement papers and drop them in the mail.

Freedom.

I didn't know that just seeing Nick's name pop up unexpectedly served as a trigger, and I'd had a textbook response to trauma. This was before the proliferation of the word. There wasn't the awareness, the language, the resources that now abound. PTSD hadn't been normalized to the point where I understood that it had to have been impacting Nick more deeply after the crash than I could know. *The Body Keeps the Score*—the bible on trauma—wasn't around at that time and would take years to become a bestseller. So, I didn't know to call this thing that stalked me "trauma." I just knew that even though I'd moved on with my life on the outside, the pain wasn't in the past—it was buried deep within, screaming with all its might to be brought to the surface.

Sam and I rarely talk about my *before*. "I forget you were even married," he says when the subject arises. *Better this way*, I think. There's an unwillingness to tread into the uncomfortable terrain of who we were or how we loved before. I carry shame. Sam carries insecurity. Or is that mine too? I hardly tell anyone about the *before*. So, I continue to exile the past, not understanding it will never exile me. Just like the depression that descends every year around the holidays. It starts around Thanksgiving—when I discovered the affair—lasts into spring, then disappears almost as quickly as it had come. I question everything about my new life: my relationship with Sam, my job, my worth. For years this happens and I never put two and two together.

I didn't know that the sting of betrayal, the violations I endured, live on in my body, stored in her vault. And it's these deep wounds to my being that still cry out for attention. As long as they sit unacknowledged, buried in the past, the trigger response happens over and over. Set off by the strangest or smallest of things: a song, the make and model of Nick's car, a military uniform, the name Christine, the smell of Crown Royal, red roses, someone sending me Nick's social media profile—*In a relationship*, it says, a new girl sitting on his lap.

Bessel van der Kolk writes, "It is one thing to process memories of trauma, but it is an entirely different matter to confront the inner void—the holes in the soul that result from not having been wanted, not having been seen, and not having been allowed to speak the truth."[3]

It's clear that I have holes in my soul that need to be reconciled, unacknowledged wounds that keep healing at bay. For now, I keep the Band-Aid on, not yet ready or willing to confront that void. But Band-Aids aren't meant to last forever. What lies underneath eventually requires attention. Removal must come.

26

INTUITION

I spot Mimi from the description she gave me as soon as she walks into the coffee shop: mid-fifties, short brown hair, a kind smile. She's interested in volunteering for the nonprofit organization I work for. After two years as a sales representative, I'd had enough of cold-calling, networking, and unfulfilling work, so I'd quit abruptly and looked for a job aligned with my master's degree in conflict resolution. I wanted meaningful work, something purposeful and passion driven. I found it at a small nonprofit that brings teenagers together from Israel, Palestine, and America for a three-week dialogue program. The first summer I volunteered, I fell in love. Mostly with the awkward, brilliant gaggle of teens who, despite their sarcasm, melted barriers with each other, finding their way right into my heart. Three months later, I was asked to become the San Diego site director. It was an incredible opportunity—the dream job I envisioned after volunteering at a refugee camp—but I quickly learned that even dream jobs have their challenges.

Mimi and I bond immediately. I feel as if I know her, and what is supposed to be an hour-long meeting quickly turns into two as we shift from the topic of volunteering to details of our personal lives.

As we near the end of the conversation, she hesitates. Somewhat self-consciously she says, "I hope I'm not overstepping here, but I need to tell you something. You need to ask for more money at your job. You're worth much more than what they are paying you. You deserve to make a comfortable living, and you don't need to give so much for so little."

I sit stunned, trying to process. *Did I give her the impression I was unhappy with work or struggling financially?*

Apologizing profusely, I ask her if I gave that impression.

She rushes to explain, "No, no . . . I saw it in your space!"

"My what?" I ask.

"Your space, your energy. The message came through crystal clear for you."

I must look confused because she attempts to explain, "My husband and I took a class on cultivating our intuition and now, whenever information comes through, I try to share the messages I receive."

I have no idea what she's talking about, but in the middle of the crowded coffee shop, I get emotional. I haven't told anyone about my financial stress, not even Sam. I've been struggling for months, stressed about every bill. Between the student loans, wedding debt, outrageous rent in San Diego, and the cost of living, I never seem to be able to catch a break. I juggle three jobs to make ends meet, but I feel tremendous guilt about negotiating a higher salary with a nonprofit. I kept telling myself the meaningful work outweighed the sacrifice. But at what expense? An invisible burden of self-doubt lifts off my shoulders. Somehow this woman, this stranger, saw what no one else had. Her seeing is the permission I didn't even know I needed.

I gather myself. "Thank you for saying that. But how did you know? What exactly did you just do?"

"Everyone has intuition," she explains, "but most people don't pay much attention to it. While it works differently for each person, there are a few ways to connect to it. It could be through sensations like sight, smell, or feeling. Some people might hear messages, while others get a visual picture of something."

She continues, "Sometimes when I'm talking to someone or doing something I'll get a message, like a flash of insight. Then I figure out how to share it with them without weirding them out. My husband is better at it than I am. When our phone rings he always knows who it is without even looking at caller ID."

She tells me about a psychic class she had taken to connect with her intuition. It sounds totally woo-woo. I'm skeptical. Then again, North County San Diego supposedly has more yoga studios per square mile than anywhere in the United States. We're obsessed with the latest health trends, willing to entertain the *far-out* if it means good skin or good vibes. I've had vitamin injections in my butt and drunk enough green juice to turn into Shrek. We have moon circles, sound baths, crystal stores, ecstatic dances, underground cults, and naked yoga. So why not a psychic class?

Reeling from her revelation and curious about her intuitive abilities, a seed is planted. I decide to sign up for the course.

We sit in a row, five chairs lined up side by side. Joni, our instructor, welcomes us to the psychic class. I glance around the dimly lit room, bewildered. There's a snow-capped man in his mid-seventies, decked out in military garb who has been attending courses for years—once upon a time, he probably stared at goats. There's a heavyset artist adorned in flaming colors with purple hair, and finally, a massage therapist in her mid-forties. I draw my attention back to Joni, with her multiple facial piercings and hands dripping in big stone rings.

Joni surveys us one by one. Her green eyes settle on mine, and she takes her time as she ominously proclaims, "This intuitive path changes things. For those of you who are in relationships, by the end of this course, you'll either be single or you will be with your partner for the rest of your life."

I look away self-consciously, thinking of Sam. *She's just being dramatic.* The incredible irony of taking a psychic course and having no idea what is to come.

27

CHOOSING ME

Four and a half years pass with Sam. We share an easy life. Skipping along the surface, content to avoid the *before*. It's not that I'm pretending; I truly love him, and he loves me. At least, as deeply as the parts we let each other see.

As couples do, we find ourselves plateauing in the realm of comfort and routine. Did the trouble start when we moved into a new apartment? A two-bedroom with more space to sequester. "I think this place is cursed," he says when we trace the discontent back. But does he not notice what I do? The partying and drinking grow old. Resentments pile up. We have the same conversations about change, with nothing to come of it. He doesn't understand my new psychic class, and I don't blame him, I hardly do myself. I finally find the courage to audition as a yoga instructor—a huge, emotional moment for me, years in the making—and when I pass, it's little more than a fleeting conversation. Sam wants children, marriage, but I still can't say with certainty that I want either. We talk less and less—or maybe we talk the same, but without saying anything that really matters. We drift apart. Something is off. I can't name it, but I feel it. And it steadily grows.

In the beginning, it didn't matter that Sam never read my blogs or showed up to my important work events. It didn't matter that he would tune me out or completely forget things I held sacred. I laughed it off when he jokingly honked at attractive women. I tolerated the comments he made about what or when I ate. I had been happy to pretend my past didn't exist. None of it mattered because I was so grateful to be loved differently than *before*. He—we—it—felt like a dream after the nightmare.

But I can no longer pretend the *before* doesn't matter. Before shouldn't be willed away, buried, denied.

"A book," I tell him. "I want to write about what I went through." I want to own my story instead of running from it, to revisit everything that transpired with Nick. The difficult process will require support and, more than anything, I want that support from Sam.

"Okay," he says, my words going in one ear and out the other like they often do, like we're leaving in ten minutes or we're ordering pizza. Not *Okay, I think that's amazing.* Not *Okay, I believe in you.* Not *Okay, that might be hard for us, but we can work through it together.* Just *Okay.*

On Saint Patrick's Day, five years after the nightmare night with Nick, I decide to post on social media about my divorce. I've never shared publicly, and the thought is petrifying. Nick and I have mutual friends from high school who will surely see. I take a deep breath at the kitchen table and close my eyes. This holiday repeatedly feels like a kick in the gut, a yearly reminder of pain. *So why now?* It feels like time. I'm ready to write, to speak.

I tap out a condensed version of what unfolded: leaving, the road trip, how wonderful life has turned out to be on the other side of that darkness. Even though I feel pride when I reflect, I'm still nervous when I hit post.

Sam comes home drunk after work and implodes. "My brother

told me about your post. What the fuck? I don't want to hear you talking about any other guys! How's that supposed to make me feel?"

I'm blindsided. Sharing had been so vulnerable, but where I'd found pride, he'd found embarrassment. He can't see past the walls of his anger, and I can't understand why he doesn't see how all that I've been through is what makes me the woman he loves. It's a huge fight that leaves me staggering. The next day is filled with apology, but the damage has been wrought.

"What if I write a whole book about my past, Sam? That was just a post and you went berserk."

"That's not fair, I was drunk. I didn't mean the things I said. If you write a book, I'll just have to get over it."

But I don't want a partner who will *just get over it*. I want a partner who, when they'd see my post, would come home, wrap me up, and tell me how proud they are.

I'm no longer satisfied to stay on the shallow surface we created, when all of me knows that I need more. More from my partner, more from life, and most of all, more from myself. It becomes increasingly clear: I haven't chosen a relationship that can hold space for my healing, perhaps because I haven't yet learned to hold that space for myself. Sam can't meet me in the place I most need to go—a place of exile. How can he? I was the one who had willingly covered her tracks and put up *No Trespassing* signs to begin with.

In psychic class we have practice readings with each other.

"Sarah," the massage therapist says with her eyes closed, "I see that whatever it is you've been avoiding is coming to the surface." *Sam. Nick. Everything.* "Are you currently in a relationship?" I confirm. "Well . . . it appears that your paths will no longer be joined. But you seem to know that already, don't you?"

In the steady but slowly encroaching discontent, my heart speaks, whispering: *It's time. You must belong to yourself first.*

It's in this growing chasm that the unexpected occurs. I begin fantasizing about being with someone else, about being single, about having a different life altogether. The desire is so strong, it takes me by surprise. It serves as a catalyst for me to be brutally honest. I'm no longer committed to our relationship, and it feels like the walls are closing in around me. I'm terrified. Am I blowing up my life? Ending a good thing? It's not like it was with Nick, where I so clearly needed to end it.

Desperate, I seek help. I get a life coach and start tapping. I start working with a shaman. I go camping alone in Sedona, hiking all day, lying awake at night. I even try meditating in an energy vortex and buy some overpriced crystals. I think about getting bangs. *Yikes.* I'm one impulsive tattoo away from changing my name to Samsara. I don't change my name, but I *do* get the tattoo, a crescent moon on my wrist. It's like someone has spiked my kombucha.

I'm terrified of hurting Sam, of making the wrong decision, of being alone. In turmoil, I confide in my new shaman. She asks, "If you had a daughter and she was in your situation, what would you want for her?"

I sit, dumbstruck. With the shift in perspective, the answer arrives effortlessly.

"I would encourage her to follow her heart, wherever it leads, regardless of the cost."

I close my eyes and finally face what I've been avoiding. Our relationship is complete. I feel the gratitude of having loved and been loved by someone like Sam, along with deep sadness. Perhaps we could have grown together instead of apart, but sometimes love is meant for a season, and he had loved me through the winter of my soul. Ours had been the necessary medicine at the perfect time, just not for all time.

The night before I end our relationship, I lie awake, sick to my stomach, dreading what is ahead. I know it'll be one of the hardest conversations I'll ever have. And it is. I hate sitting there, seeing his pain, knowing I'm the cause, hurting him to be true to me. And the worst part is when he asks, "Why?" I don't have a good answer.

How do I say what I know is true, but can't quite name? That there are parts of me that have felt banished. That over the years my life has begun to feel small. That deep down, my heart says my world is meant to be so much bigger than this life we've built in San Diego. I grasp for good reasons to be breaking his heart and the answer is just that I have to. Sam deserves to be loved in a way that I no longer do.

In the days following our breakup, I throw backpacking gear into the trunk of my new Prius and head toward the Sierras. Alone, I carry a far too heavy pack—once again—up into the John Muir Wilderness. I hang my food in a tree to elude bears. I jump into a freezing, crystal-clear lake to wash away my sweat and sins. But secretly, a little part of me wonders if I deserve to be eaten by a bear. Why does doing the right thing sometimes feel so awful?

I light a campfire at dusk; the wood turns to ash, shooting stars streaking the sky. It isn't until I'm achingly alone, a little bit afraid, and totally honest with myself that I understand, with my entire being, I did what I had to.

It never matters how we begin. Only that we do. The only thing that matters is that we have the courage to embark on the journey ahead, to the places our hearts call us to go. Even if it means wounding another to be true to ourselves. The most painful of endings can be the most beautiful of beginnings. Sometimes heartbreak is actually a homecoming. Sometimes we have to ask what we would want for the people we love to discover what we also deserve. Sometimes we have to follow our hearts, wherever they lead, regardless of the cost.

Months later, Sam will tell me he had a dream about us. We were on a boat together, floating down a river. At some point, I disembarked, leaving him to continue alone. Before we parted, I told him, "Life is just a river of love, Sam." I like to think it is.

We break the lease on our apartment. I move into a friend's spare bedroom and slowly rebuild. In my quest for healing, I try it all. *Literally all.* I continue to work with the shaman. I attend breathwork sessions and more psychic classes, I seek out mediums and card readers. I devour books on personal and spiritual development and start meditating daily. I join manifesting groups, try hypnotherapy and Reiki. I burn so much sage, I set off smoke alarms. It sounds like New Age woo-woo meets, well, more New Age woo-woo. Couldn't I have just slammed a superfood smoothie, chanted some oms, gotten a yoni egg, and called it a day? It all sounds crazy. Trust me, I know. Many of these same things I'd once condemned. But the new invitation is to be open, to ask, *Why not?* I remember: *I will be unapologetic about my healing journey.*

When I choose me and follow the whispers of my heart, I'm really saying yes to the woman I'm meant to become. A woman who is who she is because of the people she's loved, the wounds she has incurred, and all she has endured. No part of her is exiled because every part is precious. I'm saying yes to a woman who is learning to know her truth and honor when it's time to leave, that the loving and letting go along the way is a gift.

When I end my relationship with Sam, I put out to the Universe (and myself) that my next partner will be someone who has done their inner work. I know that I want to be in a healthy, nurturing partnership with someone committed to their own growth. Someone who can unequivocally support my exploration into deeper healing. Someone who values the process and is committed to their own expansion. A relationship rooted in mutual liberation.

Surrender and trust feel like the ultimate test. I love myself enough to trust myself. I trust myself enough to make the right decision. I decide from a place of wholeness. With this decision, I mend an old story and create a new future.

The Universe rewards the brave soul willing to risk it all in order to become. The path of self-reclamation demands a high price, but the gifts from the sacrifices along the way become the dream I hadn't yet dared to dream.

28

FULL CIRCLE

I look out at the bodies stretched on their mats before me. From the back of the studio, I see my reflection in the mirror. I no longer look away self-consciously; instead, I feel a swell of pride. I project my voice. "Savasana, our final pose. There's nothing else to do. Nowhere else to be. No more effort required. Just breathe and be. Honor this space between your practice and the rest of your day."

My voice trails off as I walk around the room. Stopping above one of the students, I gently push her shoulders down. She visibly softens as I lift her neck, extend her spine, and set her head back down. I adjust others and make my way to my mat.

I sit cross-legged and wait a few minutes. I take a moment and remember what it took to get here.

The very first hot yoga class I ever attempted, hiding in the back, fumbling my way through. The confident instructor—Lise—who gave me the gift of feeling safe in my body and getting honest with myself. How never in my wildest dreams did I imagine that one day I would be her, guiding class and holding space for others on their mats.

I had some illusion that I needed to be perfect in order to teach.

There was some imagined destination where I would arrive and all of a sudden, I would have the courage, confidence, and ability to guide a class. I thought it took being someone other than who I was, a version of myself that was more self-assured, more knowledgeable, further along in her own practice. These beliefs kept me small. I sat behind a desk in a yoga studio for two years—checking people in, cleaning bathrooms, folding towels—instead of stepping into the role my heart told me I was capable of. I had my certification; the only thing holding me back . . . was me. I was petrified of rejection, of not being good enough.

I finally realized it isn't about being perfect, it's about being authentic. I'll never be a flawlessly toned yogi who can hold a handstand or sit in full lotus like annoying spandex lady. Not even close. I can't say all the poses in Sanskrit, and I certainly can't name all the muscles that are contracting or expanding as we move. But I can show up with what I know. And I know that yoga is so much more than a workout. It broke me open and taught me how to be strong. It gave me my confidence back, and that doesn't stop at the studio door. Yoga helped me do life better. And to share something I love, something that fundamentally changed me . . . I can't think of a bigger honor. Maybe that's also why it terrifies me, showing up as a work in progress and trusting that I'm enough.

For the audition to become an instructor, I'd memorized the sequence for hours. I was only a few minutes in when the manager cut me off. "Are you kidding? You *so* have this!" I was both elated and panicked because that meant it would be real, that my name would be on the schedule. In that first class I taught my voice was shaky, my body trembling with nerves and excitement. Of course, I made mistakes, but I also learned to laugh about them, to not take myself so damn seriously. I think back to the spiritual yoga training that led me here. How Christian friends had ominously warned me before the course, "Be careful, Sarah May, don't lose your faith."

My whole life, and especially in my marriage, religion was the tether I desperately clung to. I was raised in the Church. Youth group on Thursdays, sermons every Sunday. I went to a conservative Christian college where classes on the Bible were required. Drinking and dancing were forbidden. Dorms had "open hours" when boys could visit. Even then, they couldn't use the bathroom and had to have their feet firmly planted on the floor at all times. Premarital sex was probably just about as taboo as taking a psychic class—that is to say, a big, fat, wicked no-no.

I'd been uncomfortable in the yoga program when they spoke about things like chakras, astrology, energy, karma, and reincarnation. I listened respectfully but dismissed them readily. These concepts didn't fit within the confines of my religion. If anything, they were occult. Yet the discomfort did something powerful—it ushered in questions. That bristling had been a crack in the door, the first time I'd asked: *Which of the things I was taught and told to believe actually resonate with me? How and where have I experienced God on my own?*

At first, I'd felt disloyal, a traitor to my cause, like I was doing something wrong by even questioning. But I learned to call the beliefs I was raised with my "inherited beliefs" and that inheriting something didn't mean I needed to keep it. On the other side of a religious upbringing that never quite resonated, the process of questioning was everything.

Why is a powerful initiator. *Why* ushers a critical invitation: *Choose my beliefs instead of simply consuming them.* I found very quickly that connection to God *for me* wasn't taking communion or getting baptized. It wasn't sitting in a pew or cracking open a hymnal.

But I faced judgment and criticism. People were concerned about my soul going down a path of damnation since their religious way was the *only way*. It was a lonely place, but it was a truer place, and that was enough to fuel my fire.

Renowned author and shame researcher, Dr. Brené Brown writes in *The Gifts of Imperfection* that: "Spirituality is recognizing and celebrating that we are all inextricably connected to each other by a power greater than all of us, and that our connection to that power and to one another is grounded in love and compassion. . . . Spirituality brings a sense of perspective, meaning, and purpose . . ."[5]

Over time, I've discovered that sense of perspective, purpose, and meaning. I've found the places where I experience God. It's in the safe confines of a yoga studio, surrounded by people breathing and moving, creating something beautiful together. This has become my worship. It's out in the wild, surrounded by trees and mountains and rivers, dirt underneath my bare feet. This has become my sanctuary. It's in community, surrounded by kind people who love big and give generously and who care about making a positive impact. This has become my congregation. It's in my daily journaling and meditation practice, with the invitation to be still and know. This has become my communion.

The words from my Christian friends come back to me . . . *Don't lose your faith*. In the end, I didn't lose it. For the first time in my life, I genuinely found it. It was waiting for me in the *why*. It found me on my yoga mat. Crying, fumbling, becoming.

Why makes for the most powerful awakening of all: the questioning of everything to arrive at a faith based on resonance within the soul, peace within the heart, and ease within the being. I've reconciled with the God of the institution and the God within my own heart. We have a deeply personal relationship cultivated by the courage to question everything I was taught to believe. For me, there isn't a singular road map to the divine. I like to believe there are a million paths that can be true as long as they lead back to love.

I remember my own path back to love as I look out at the bodies before me. Sweaty and silent. In closing, I guide them out of Savasana. We sit cross-legged, our hands in prayer position, eyes closed.

My voice carries across the room. "My soul honors your soul. I honor the place in you where the entire Universe resides. I honor the light, love, truth, beauty, and peace within you, because it's also within me. In sharing these things, we are united, we are one. Namaste."

A sweet chorus of voices respond, "Namaste."

I breathe it in so I can remember.

29

LINGERING

Students roll up their mats as a rising sun shines through the blinds. It's early, 7:00 a.m., but I'm wide awake after teaching another hot yoga class. I stand outside, thanking people for coming and seeing them off. When I go to clean the room, one student is still lingering, taking his time.

"Another great class," says Andrew (A.) with a smile. The grin stretches across his handsome face, leaving little crow's-feet next to striking blue eyes. His auburn hair is parted to the side. Stubble traces a sharp jawline. Shirtless, A.'s skin glistens from the heat, his torso toned and lean. At six feet, his tall frame dwarfs my five-foot, two-inch (five three on a good day) posture. His body drips sweat with a steady *drip, drip, drip* on the floor. The studio is heated to 105 degrees with 50 percent humidity. It would be strange if he *wasn't* sweating profusely.

"Thanks!" I respond, fidgeting with the stereo. "How's your week been?"

A.'s been coming to my class every week for the past six months. We'd met back in March, when I was still with Sam. He'd hung around after that first class and casually mentioned surfing together.

Had he been asking me out? I'd brushed it off, avoiding my relationship status, and the moment passed. We'd talked about other things. It had been friendly and it stayed that way. He hadn't asked me out again, and over the following months—my consequent breakup with Sam and moving out—A. and I had grown into an easy friendship. His presence had become a trend. Week after week, month after month, he'd roll out his mat like clockwork, then linger for post-class conversation. Today is no different.

He fills me in on his work as a teacher at an international school as I grab a mop and start to spray disinfectant on the wet floor. I laugh when he tells me about his roomie's latest dating dramas. "Roomie" is his ninety-two-year-old grandpa who is on-again, off-again with his girlfriend.

"And what about your book? How's it coming?" I ask. A.'s accomplished what I still dream of doing. He's written a book and is trying to get it published.

As usual, there is no shortage of conversation between us. A. has road-tripped across the country—twice—and we swap stories of hiking, camping, and backpacking. When I don't see him for a week or two, he'll return with tales about renting a van in Iceland and hiking volcanoes in the midnight sun. Another time, he tells me about a week spent in Croatia at a music festival, dancing for days on end completely sober. Each week, time dwindles faster than the week before. Before I know it, I'm smiling goodbye and seeing him out the studio door.

One Friday, I announce I'll no longer be teaching the early morning class. The commute from my new apartment is no longer feasible. I'm exhausted from juggling three jobs, and waking up at 4:30 a.m. has become unbearable. After the announcement, A. approaches me post-class, visibly disappointed. "I'm so bummed. I'm going to really miss your class," he says. "Maybe we can get together next week instead? Catch a sunset at the beach?"

This time, I do not brush it off. I say yes.

We sit facing one another on a blanket while the last of the setting sun lights up the sky with gold hues. Small waves break on the shore where the last of the surfers pay their tribute to the swell.

A. looks at me. "One time in class you said something I'm curious about. You said yoga saved your life . . . Can you tell me more?"

I'm temporarily caught off guard; it's a big question with a vulnerable answer. I dig my feet into the sand, watch the waves, and slowly begin to tell my story. It comes out disjointed. I realize that in the last several years, I've only told a handful of people. But I hold nothing back as A. listens intently, his body leaning toward mine. When I finish, he breathes out heavily.

"Wow . . . I never would've guessed you've been through so much. It sounds like a Lifetime movie. I mean we've been friends for six months and I had no clue. I'm honored you trust me with your story."

His blue eyes bore into mine. Something about it makes me feel both deeply seen and simultaneously naked, like I've just shown him my soul and he's calling it beautiful. The intensity makes me look away. Self-conscious, I laugh it off. "And what about you? What's your story?"

The sun disappears on the horizon. Dusk falls across the expanse of ocean before us, twilight ushering in purples and violets with the first glimmering of stars.

A. clears his throat. "I think I mentioned I'm sober?"

I nod.

"Well I got sober at twenty-four . . . So, nine years ago. On the outside, you could have labeled me a functioning alcoholic. Degree, job, lease, girlfriend, all that crap. But honestly, I don't know a single functioning adult who would have considered my behavior anything other than dysfunctional and insane.

"I blacked out a lot, and vomited most days of the week. I binge drank, and lived that way for a while. Either drunk or hungover. My rock bottom dragged on for months. My poor ex-girlfriend, all the drama I caused. And my poor mom, she developed ulcers worrying about me. It wasn't until I had my own health scare that I woke up. The doctors thought I had cancer, and it took weeks until they concluded that it was just the damage all the drinking had caused. So, when my doctor told me I had to stop drinking, I knew I couldn't do it on my own. I went and got help and I've been sober ever since."

"Oh my gosh . . . you've got quite the story yourself," I say, in awe of his honesty. A. is the first recovered alcoholic to share their story with me. I know little about the world of sobriety; my own consumption of alcohol has been largely unquestioned. "So, what ended up happening with your health?" I ask.

"When I quit drinking, it improved drastically. But getting sober was the hardest thing I've ever done. I had terrible withdrawals. It was the Twelve Steps that truly transformed me. At first, I was going to meetings every day, sometimes two or three. Now, I go once or twice a week. I get to take other guys struggling through the Steps. I guess kinda like how you get to share yoga with others."

"Wow. That's amazing."

"But I want to be honest . . ." A.'s tone shifts as he looks away. There's an increased vulnerability in the air when he speaks. "I haven't dated in a while. I have a bit of . . . commitment phobia. I didn't think much of it until earlier this year when I was diagnosed with panic disorder. I was having panic attacks from dating. Well, not like asking women out, or being nervous on dates. But the deeper stuff, the emotional intimacy. Anytime things progressed or I needed to set some boundaries, my anxiety worsened. I would try and have the difficult conversations, but that only made the panic attacks worse. Eventually, they got so bad that I thought I was going to have to quit my job. Even after I stopped dating, the panic never went away. So, I started going to therapy earlier this year."

"Really?" I ask, interested. *A man in therapy? Green flag.* "How's your mental health now?"

"It's better. I have an amazing therapist and we're still working together, and I haven't had a panic attack in a couple of months."

When he finishes, I thank him for sharing. If I just got naked with my vulnerability, he stripped down too. I can't recall the last time—if ever—a man has been so forthright, so transparent about his struggles. The openness between us feels raw, true, brave. It's both unnerving and invigorating.

Long after the sun has set, A. walks me back to my car. I slip into the driver's seat as he holds the door. Sand on my toes, a smile on my face, a glow remaining.

⸻

Several nights later, a girlfriend and I go to an indie dance party downtown. Amidst the dark of the club and the throbbing of the bass, I see a familiar face. It's A. *What are the chances?* It isn't long before we spot each other and he makes his way over.

"Hey!" he shouts over the music.

I smile wide. "I had no idea you'd be here!"

"Likewise! Are you alone?"

"Just with my one friend. You?"

"Same."

We introduce our friends to each other, who already seem to know this won't be the night out they originally intended. I motion to my girlfriend and tell A., "We're going to head deeper into the dance floor if you wanna join?"

"Sure!" he exclaims, tailing close behind as we thread our way into a mass of bodies.

For a stone-cold sober thirty-something, A. dances like a maniac. I love it. I meet him in a wild frenzy. He quickly sweats through his T-shirt as a circle forms, our friends moving off to the side. We shake and shimmy song after song. Dancing, laughing, singing. There are strobe lights and fog machines, disco balls and bass. His blue eyes are trained on mine; my hands are around his neck. Our faces grow closer and closer. And then . . . tippy toes, closed eyes, crashing lips.

In the weeks that follow, A. and I bare our hearts to one another. We talk about our recent struggles and in the next breath laugh over his impersonations and goofy sense of humor. He loves to cook, and usually does so serenading me with a spatula to Boyz II Men or Barry White. He makes a playlist for our date night and titles it *No, I Don't Do This for Every Girl*, burning me a CD of the playlist like we're still in high school. He takes me to the planetarium, then pretends to be interested when I read him his astrological birth chart. Imagine: a tattooed white girl with a nose ring explaining how compatible Pisces and Virgo are and he barely flinches. He even puts up with the disgusting yak sounds I make when I don't like something, and the way I sometimes act like I have an answer to everything (when in fact I have no idea what I'm talking about). We go to yoga together, and in Savasana, I feel his fingers wrap around mine as we lie side by side. His sobriety leads me to question my own relationship with alcohol—one that has fueled countless harmful decisions and relationship drama—and I begin my own sober-curious commitment. We hike the nearby mountain together, where I tell A. about my own dreams to write a book. He stops mid-step and looks at me.

"Sarah . . . that's amazing. Your story is so powerful. How can I support you?"

I'm so moved that I'm temporarily speechless. "You just did," is all I can say.

But as things escalate between us, so too does my insecurity about entertaining this new romance. I struggle to admit there hasn't been a lot of time between ending things with Sam and saying yes to A. I wrestle with the socially acceptable notion of appropriate timing between relationships. I'm faced with my own projections and expectations as I overcome judgments, both real and perceived from others. Not that I'm proud of it or think it's healthy, but I tend to jump from one relationship to the next.

Call it rationalization, but I decide it's not how much time that has passed that matters, it's the work I have done and will continue to do along the way. I'm conscious of my fears of betrayal and abandonment triggered by intimacy. I know all too well my codependent tendencies. I'm aware there is a part of me, truthfully a large part, that loves to feel wanted, even if there are glaring red flags. I've chosen being charmed over being truly seen and known. I wanted a partner who wouldn't be uncomfortable or threatened by my past, by my story, and now that it's a real possibility, the resulting vulnerability is completely foreign.

As I learn who A. is—a man of incredible integrity—there's no question, I want to see where things can lead. Timeline be damned. His commitment to recovery and continued personal work inspire me. No part of me is exiled, no topic is taboo; if anything, he encourages me to go deeper, to draw nearer to my wounds. Instead of a Band-Aid, our relationship becomes a supportive and safe place for excavation. Having a partner is no prerequisite for healing, but being with someone who unequivocally supports doing the work is a gift more valuable than gold.

When I finally receive a call back from the therapist I've been pestering for an appointment, I request her first available slot. It's time. Time to venture to the places that terrify me. To unearth that which has been buried. To face all that has been suppressed. Wounds fully exposed to the light, ready for examination.

30

RECONCILING

It was during yoga teacher training when I first heard the words *marital rape*. I'd shared the raw story of everything that had transpired with Nick to my closest friends, Cielo and Jan. Still processing everything myself, I had hardly confided in anyone.

"That morning was the last time I had sex with my husband," I told them, but the words felt wrong. Silence filled the parked car before Cielo spoke.

"Sarah," she said gravely, "that is marital rape. You were raped."

At the time, I denied it. It felt like too serious of an accusation. It was too soon for me to be honest, even with myself. Denial is a sick person's best friend, and I had the most loyal of companions. Now, six years after that conversation with Cielo, memories that were once hazy have come into sharp focus. *What really happened that morning?*

Why go back? Because truth deserves awareness and what we don't own, owns us. Because even though time has passed, it doesn't simply heal the wound. Because when I think about that morning, I instinctively feel that something was deeply and dreadfully wrong.

I sit across from my therapist in a small, stuffy room. Blonde-haired, brown-eyed, petite and unfailingly stylish, Diane and I have been meeting for weekly sessions for a while now. The air is warm and I fidget on the cream couch trying to get comfortable.

"I remember when it happened that I was crying and saying no," I confide to Diane. "But I feel like I could have fought against it harder…" I pause, collecting myself, averting my gaze.

"He was so familiar to me. Having sex was a huge part of our relationship, how we showed love. But at the time it was so confusing. I was so numb and in so much shock after discovering his next affair. Not to mention the terror of talking him down from pulling the trigger . . . It was like my body knew him intimately and wanted to respond like it did all the other times, but I hated him so much in that moment. I didn't understand why he was doing it—it was the last thing I wanted and the very last thing in the world that made any sense to me."

I clear my throat as I try to find the words. This part is the hardest for me to admit. I can't look up. "I feel like my body betrayed me . . ."

And there it is—the dirty secret I've been carrying. It's the shame burning a hole through my conscience. My body had responded to Nick's advances even though every single fiber of my being did not want what was unfolding. She responded with a *yes* when everything in me was screaming *no*.

"Sarah," Diane says softly, "it's very clear what happened was not consensual. In the confines of marriage, consent is still necessary. You said no and he proceeded anyway. Even if you hadn't said no, there were still multiple indicators that sent clear signals of non-consent—from your body language, emotional reaction, and vulnerable state. He took advantage of you. It's very common for survivors to blame themselves and feel shame. Especially when there is a physical response. But let me be perfectly clear, what happened was assault and not okay."

I breathe out heavily and consider. I'd said, "I don't want this," but I didn't scratch his eyes out when he peeled off my pants. I was crying, but I didn't scream when he pulled off his. Those hands that had once brought me so much pleasure, the man who had once worshipped my body . . . all to be rendered powerless, brought so low, made so small. There would be no reconciling. Only a dissonance. Only hot tears streaming down an anguished face. Where was my fire? Where was my fight?

I didn't yet know that one of the most common responses to being sexually assaulted is to freeze. That the fear, shock, and confusion can be immobilizing. In that moment, I shut down. My voice little more than a whisper, my attempts feeble. I just couldn't grasp what was happening.

Jon Krakauer's book *Missoula* features a forensic consultant who specializes in sexual assault, Dr. David Lisak, who says, "Victims of non-stranger rape are often very confused about what happened. They may be very upset. But they don't automatically label what's happened to them as rape. In fact, there's a lot of research about this. It's not uncommon for victims to go back and forth between feeling like something really bad happened to them, and being very confused, and even trying to deny that something bad happened to them."[6]

That was me. At the time, *I'm being raped* never entered my mind, even though what was happening was a clear violation. It would take six years of denial to finally name what transpired. It didn't help that I was ignorant about rape. I thought rapists were strangers who followed you to your car, broke into your apartment, or drugged you.

This can and does happen, but an overwhelming majority of rapes, an estimated 85 percent, are committed by an acquaintance.[7]

Even knowing what I know now, I still carry shame about my body's physical reaction. Mostly, I carry confusion. *Why would Nick do that to me?*

I finally meet Diane's gaze. My entire body is tense as I perch on the edge of the couch.

"Why?" I struggle to get the words out. "Why did he do that to me?"

Diane considers for a moment. "When he did that, you'd just finished telling him you were done, that it was over between you, correct?"

I nod.

"I see it as his final way of exerting power over you. His last act of control when he felt that he was finally losing you."

I sit silent, turning this new understanding over in my mind. Nick had used my vulnerable state and naked body as a form of power and control. What he had done was not love, it was assault. By all definitions, it was rape.

I sigh heavily and fall back into the couch.

It's called non-concordance, and naming it gives me immense relief. My body may have responded to physical stimuli, but it did not mean that I wanted or enjoyed what had happened. Diane's validation helps to eradicate the shame. I felt worthless underneath the man I once trusted and loved as my pleas were met with silence, as my resistance went ignored. I felt degraded, an empty shell of a human. I could have melted into the puddle of tears beneath me and dissolved away. By naming the violation, the dissonance fades. There is no more confusion, no more excuses, no more denial.

Cielo's words from yoga teacher training all those years earlier land at a time and place where I can finally hear them. The truth was always beneath the surface. I dive into unexplored terrain, having never visited because I couldn't call it what it was. But the body is a vessel that holds memory, and she remembers all.

A few weeks after the insights from therapy, I'm lying down on a yoga mat spread across the grass. I pull a beanie over my eyes. India, a breathwork instructor, is a petite brunette with soft brown eyes, a large nose ring, and various tattoos splashed across her arms. I like her immediately. She's empathetic and spunky. I'm with a small group of girlfriends, spread out in a backyard on a Sunday afternoon.

India explains, "Transformational breathwork is a powerful modality that utilizes a certain breathing technique to oxygenate the body and facilitate the release of suppressed emotions, tension, and blockages."

I fidget, pulling a blanket up to my chin as I pay close attention to India's instructions. "This is an open mouth breathing technique. Pull in deep, big, powerful inhales, all the way down into your belly. Feel your belly expand completely, then bring your breath up into your chest. Finally, release with a soft, quick, silent exhale. Make the exhale last only a second or two." My mouth wide open, I focus on my breath, finding the rhythm: belly, chest, release; belly, chest, release. "Relax your body, your shoulders. See if you can sink down into the earth beneath you," she says.

I can tell by the sound of her voice that she's moving around the circle, monitoring everyone's chests as they rise and fall. A few minutes later, a tingling sensation stirs in my fingers; a buzz courses through my veins as my body becomes more oxygenated. India presses play on the speaker and music washes over us. I find my pace: belly, chest, release.

Softer now, India invites us into the experience. "I'm safe to be in my body. It's safe to feel." I follow her words and stay with the deep breathing. With my eyes closed, the blackness starts to take on forms as my entire body hums with electric vibrations. India tells us that this type of breathing can induce an altered state of consciousness.

Like a movie in my mind's eye, scenes from my wedding day form. It's crystal clear: the way the sun and moon hung in the sky at the same time, the light dazzling off the water, lines of white chairs filled with family and friends. At the end of the sandy aisle is Nick, his brown eyes fixed on mine. We hold hands at the altar. I still hear India facilitating as she moves around the circle. I know where my body lies in physical space, but my mind is a world away, taking me back to years before, reliving the ceremony in vivid detail.

From across the circle, India says, "We're going to make some noise together. Take the deepest inhale you can, bring in as much air as possible . . . sip in even more, fill all the way up."

My chest expands, my lungs filled with oxygen. "When you're ready," she prompts, "scream! Yell! Let all your emotions out! Let it go! Shake your body, stomp your feet, bang your fists into the ground! Whatever is coming out, whatever you've denied, let it out now!"

I think of Nick. Of the violation to my body. With her urging, I let go of my breath and scream. I yell as loud as I can while I pound my fists into the mat underneath me. "AGH!!!!" When I run out of air, she has us do it again. Then again. Each time we grow louder. My body grows hot as anger—so much anger—bubbles to the surface.

"Good!" India exclaims. "Now . . . hold your breath. Hold it for as long as you can. When you think you can't, hold it just a little longer."

I suck in cool air, deep into my lungs, filling my chest, and sealing my lips. When I do, the vision from before grows stronger. Nick and

I's first kiss, the taste of his lips, the smell of his cologne. Our smiles as they announce us at the reception and we walk in the room. Our first dance as husband and wife. Nick twirls me then pulls me in so my back is against his chest as we sway to one of our favorite songs. His hands are on my hips with only the thin silk of my wedding dress separating our touch.

In one world I'm there, but in the other I feel India approach. She pushes her fingers down into my hip joints and quietly, so that only I can hear, she prods, "It's safe to feel."

Her touch feels just like Nick's. She pushes harder. "It's safe to be in my body. I can let go." Nick is holding me, his hands on my waist, his body against mine. The pressure builds from India's fingers. Instantaneously, the vision changes. What was our first dance as husband and wife becomes the very last time I felt my husband's hands on my hips.

His weight is pushing down on top of me. The softness of our old couch beneath me sinks under the pressure. He smells like alcohol. Sunlight streams through the windows. My yellow-and-turquoise pajama pants are at my ankles. I can't bring myself to look at him. I tell him no, but it unfolds anyway. I do not want this.

In the world where I have grass underneath me and it is India, not Nick, applying pressure, I lose my breath. Hot tears squeeze themselves out of the corners of my eyes, leaking from underneath my beanie. In a soft whisper, India urges, "It's okay. You're safe now. Let it go."

So I do. The tears slide down my cheeks as heavy sobs wrack my body. I cry for all the times I didn't, for the violations to my heart and body and mind. I cry for the space between my first dance with my husband and the last time I felt his hands on my hips. Tears fall until we know that I am safe, that I can trust myself. Dry heaves fill my chest and I know that something has been released, deep, deep down in my body.

A new scene unfolds. I see our wedding, but this time I'm not in it; I'm safely floating above it. Nick disappears. I'm at the end of the aisle, holding my own hands, transfixed by my own eyes, saying *yes* to me. Then, I see our apartment. I watch, like a ghost, the very last time my husband touched my naked body. I see me there, underneath him; how when it's all over, we sit like strangers on opposite ends of the couch. I take my hands and lead myself out of that place. I close the door behind us. I hold myself in my arms, wipe away my tears, and tell us: *What happened was wrong and we never, ever have to go back. We're safe now. I love you.*

With that shutting of the door I know, in both worlds, that I can hold it all. Love and rage. Betrayal and forgiveness. Gratitude and grief. Joy and pain. From the first dance to the last moment, I know now I can hold it all. So I do. I breathe in. I let it go.

31

ABANDONED

In each of my sweaty hands, I hold small, electric buzzers. A vibration shoots through my left palm.

"Can you feel it?" Diane asks as the sensation subsides. I nod from my seat across from her, balancing on the edge of the couch. A text lights up my phone. I glance at it briefly and my heart does a little leap.

A.: I'm so proud of you. Be gentle with yourself after. I hope it's a productive session.

I silence the phone while Diane explains the process. "The buzzing will alternate in each of your palms. I'll ask you to focus on your anchor memory. In other words, the traumatic moment you're wanting to process. Bring it to life, recall it as vividly as possible, like you're really back in there. For two minutes see where it takes you. I'll tell you when the round is complete and we'll process together."

This is my first time doing Eye Movement Desensitization and Reprocessing (EMDR), a type of therapy that can be especially effective for processing trauma. I was intrigued after hearing about A.'s insights with his own therapist. With the support of a trained professional, traumatic memories are recalled and reprocessed with the assistance of sensory (sight or sensation) cues. The process dismantles the memories' hold on the body and subconscious, allowing for deep neural reprogramming.

"Okay," she says from her chair across the room, "let's begin."

I close my eyes. With her prompting, I visualize the apartment I shared with Nick. The tan sectional couch, the cream carpet, the black credenza, the furniture we picked out together at World Market, the granite countertops in the kitchen.

The buzzer vibrates in my palms, alternating from left to right. The rational part of my brain tells me I'm sitting with my therapist, six years later in San Diego, in a safe place. But the feelings and emotions stored in my body are not as rational. Just visualizing spikes my heart rate, sending shock waves through my nervous system.

Gently, Diane asks, "Where do you feel it in your body?"

My chest feels constricted, my breath shallow. Armor has been placed around my core to defend it from this siege of emotion. "My heart," I croak back.

"Do you want to continue?"

I nod.

"What are you doing in the apartment? What's happening?"

I open the door to our bedroom and make my way to Nick's side of the bed. He always slept on the left. But it's been a few days since the shape of his body has taken up space there. I look down at the bedside table, tracing my fingers along the dark, smooth grain.

I second-guess myself with this EMDR process. My mind isn't taking me back to the night things imploded, but before. As the memory unfolds, it becomes clear that this had taken place when we were temporarily separated. I was living alone in the apartment, holding out disillusioned hope he would come back. I voice my doubts to Diane who urges me onward, "Keep going with it. Let's see where it takes you."

In the confines of our bedroom, I stand above the bedside table and slowly slide open the drawer. A shooting stab hits my gut. There, sitting in the drawer, tossed aside and abandoned, is my husband's wedding ring. The glint of gold in the afternoon light, the unmistakable engraving on the back side. It has been left in secret, left in the dark. Tossed in next to old letters and notebooks, pens and loose change. Left with things that didn't matter. Things he would never come back to. *How long?* I wonder. *How long ago did he take it off and throw it in here?*

I glance down at my left hand where my own wedding ring hangs heavy. I still haven't given up. I couldn't yet know he'd taken off his ring for romantic rendezvous with Christine. At the sight of it in the drawer, my hope dwindles to despair. If the gold could talk, it would mock me: *Silly girl, can't you see how he's flung you aside?* An abandoned promise tucked away to be forgotten, the symbol of our sacred vows thoughtlessly discarded.

The hurt is a raw ache in my heart, an open gash that spills its poison of rejection so deep it becomes a moment I consciously choose to forget. I close the drawer softly. Turning, I walk out of the bedroom. The place we made love, fought, and dreamed, perhaps of each other, perhaps of others. The place he left his broken promise. The final place we shared as husband and wife never to return to.

The vibration in my right palm jolts me back to the present. I've been so lost in memory that I haven't felt the sting of tears that now slide down my cheeks. It takes me a minute to compose myself as Diane hands me a box of tissues.

"Where did the memory take you?" she asks softly.

I wipe my eyes and recount the unsettling discovery. "I haven't thought of that moment since it happened. I don't even know where that came from. I've never told anyone about it. When it happened, I knew deep down that something was wrong, but I was still in denial, hoping he would come back."

The tears keep flowing as I feel, for the very first time, the wound that moment inflicted. It arrives now, undeniable: *abandonment*.

Diane explains, "Often times with EMDR you'll have an anchor memory, but other memories or feelings may surface. Think of it like a spiderweb that comprises a neural network in your brain. What came up is attached to your anchor memory. It's all connected—this process is like following a map. As we heal and process what you shared, we're also working on the anchor memory. Everything you see and experience has a purpose. It's being brought to the surface for a reason. Really good job."

I take a deep breath and wipe away another tear.

"Are you ready to go back in?" she asks.

I close my eyes and nod. The buzzers vibrate in my palms.

I learn that I was enmeshed with Nick in a trauma bond relationship. Trauma bonds are categorized by early, strong affection, grand gestures, possessiveness veiled as caring, and turbulent highs and lows. His acting out through betrayal, manipulation, and threats was followed by empty promises to be better, do better, and never again. The intensity of shared emotional experience created a deep attachment that became difficult to leave. There was no agency, no sense of self-autonomy. He couldn't show up for me because he could barely face himself. I couldn't enforce boundaries because I didn't have the self-respect to honor them. If I didn't think I was enough, how could I ever say "Enough!"?

Maybe at the time we didn't know any other way, both young, lonely, desperate. The abandonment I felt from Nick cut deeply, but I realize that in trying to save him, to be enough for him, I was really *abandoning myself.*

Glennon Doyle writes in *Untamed*: "Maybe the question was no longer *How could he have done this to me?* but *How can I keep doing this to myself?* Maybe instead of forever repeating, *How could he have abandoned me?* I needed to ask, *Why do I keep abandoning myself?*"[8]

According to the Oxford Dictionary, *abandon* means "to cease to support or look after." I discovered on the winding trails of Bryce that I had lost myself in the identity of being a wife. Not consciously, but one day I looked up and no longer recognized who I was or what my life had become. Abandonment is different. Like secretly tossing a wedding ring in a drawer when still married, ceasing to look after what it symbolizes. Abandonment is a conscious giving away, a conceding in the face of small battles that eventually add up to the entire war.

How did I cease to look after myself? In the things I resented but did anyway. In the apologizing, even though I had no reason to be saying sorry. It was thinking I needed to pick my battles, so I buried valid feelings in an attempt to save energy for the bigger inevitable fights. I tolerated verbal and at times, physical abuse because I believed him when he apologized the next day, desperately holding out hope there wouldn't be a next time. I believed his lies, even after he gave me every reason not to. I stayed. I don't have to look far to see how I codependently adapted to placate him.

I caught him reading my journal one afternoon. My most sacred place, completely violated. It was an intrusion like none other. It seemed that nowhere was safe. I demanded that he never do it again, but he did. Eventually, I stopped demanding and started withholding on the page, monitoring my words for what might cause him insecurity or jealousy. I stopped telling the truth for the sake of love. I see now how wrong it all was, how the most important things were violated one by one: my journal, my heart, my trust, my body.

No, I was not lost. I'd ceased to look after myself. The pain of being abandoned by another cuts deep, but abandoning the self inflicts an agony that *must* be reconciled.

I discover Dr. Lindsay Gibson's *Adult Children of Emotionally Immature Parents*, and its contents rock me to the core. No book has validated me so deeply or helped me integrate the scope of my experience with Nick—and where I come from—so profoundly. Understanding why and how things transpired the way they did has helped me find peace. When terrible things happened and I struggled to make sense of the *why*, Gibson's pages help make meaning.

Dr. Gibson differentiates between two types of personalities that emerge in children when one or both parents are emotionally immature. Children learn to cope with emotional deprivation by either internalizing their problems or externalizing them. She explains:

"Because of their attunement to others, they (internalizers) can get so focused on other people's issues that they lose sight of their own needs and overlook how the emotional drain is harming them. In addition, they are secretly convinced that more self-sacrifice and emotional work will eventually transform their unsatisfying relationships. So, the greater the difficulties, the more they try. . . . Because internalizers look within themselves for reasons why things go wrong, they may not always recognize abuse for what it is. . . . It's hard for internalizers to give up the fight to be loved, but sometimes they eventually realize that they can't single-handedly change how another person relates to them. They finally feel resentment and begin to withdraw emotionally. When an internalizer ultimately does give up, the other person may be caught off guard, since the internalizer had continued to reach out and try to connect for so long."[9]

It's like Gibson psychoanalyzed me and put me on the page better than I could have myself. Why I stayed, hoped, fought. Why, at the time, I never would have categorized Nick's behavior as abusive. And why, when I told him I was done, he was surprised, thinking I would still be waiting. She continues:

"In contrast to internalizers, externalizers act out their anxiety, pain, or depression. They do impulsive things to distract themselves from their immediate problems. Although this may help them feel better temporarily, it creates more problems down the road. When externalizers have to face the consequences of their impulsivity, they're vulnerable to strong but brief feelings of shame and failure. However, they usually use denial to avoid shame, rather than wondering whether or how they might need to change. This lands them in a vicious cycle of impulsivity followed by feelings of failure that prompt still more impulsivity. . . . To avoid total self-hatred, they rid themselves of shame by blaming others and making excuses. . . . Needy externalizers tend to pursue warm and giving internalizers. Initially, they make the internalizer feel special in order to secure the relationship, but once they have the person, they stop doing the emotional work of reciprocating. The internalizers are surprised at this turnaround, and often blame themselves."[9]

There is a click in my brain as the puzzle pieces fall into place. I'm able to understand my behavior for what it was, name Nick's patterns, and see clearly the roles we both played and *why*.

As I acknowledge my part in our story, I see that *who* and *what* I chose spoke infinitely more about me than what had happened to me. In so many ways, I was just a little girl looking to be saved. A little boy had come along and taken my hand. I didn't trust myself, so I placed my trust in him. We played adults, pretending we could fix each other, and made one of the biggest decisions of our lives on a foundation made of sand. I see it all, and I have so much compassion for that little girl and little boy.

I grieve for that little girl who abandoned herself for another. I grieve for my marriage, built on wounds, never destined to last. I grieve for those who also know that very specific and terrible kind of pain: the ceasing of looking after the self at the expense of the heart. Through this work, I go back for that little girl. She and I have a homecoming.

This work is clearing the rubble to make space for new development. We are both the architect and excavator of the landscape within. Creating a sustainable sense of self involves building a strong foundation from the inside out. The beautiful thing about acknowledging self-abandonment is the invitation to begin again, to provide support to spaces that were suppressed or denied, to give adequacy to inadequacy, to fill the internal well with deservingness and love. The self is the only thing we have for a lifetime. We are the one we need, the very one we've been waiting for.

The question becomes: *Where did I learn this abandonment from?*

32

ANCESTORS

Three months into my infancy, Mom noticed my father crying while he changed my diaper. Alarmed, she asked what was wrong.

"I'm just sad," he responded vaguely.

Later that day, she was called to their pastor's office where Dad was waiting. He confessed the unthinkable: He'd contracted a sexually transmitted disease from a sex worker and admitted that he'd been struggling with sex addiction for the last seventeen years. Keeping his secret had passed the point of silence with the diagnosis. He'd always promised himself that if it ever came to jeopardizing her health, he'd come clean.

She was devastated, betrayed, and humiliated. Her best friend, father of her children, and husband of eighteen years had broken their vows and her heart. Still, she had a newborn, a family to raise. My mother loved him. His apologies were desperate and sincere. He was willing to do anything to make the marriage work, vowing, "I will do whatever I can to help you, for us to get through this."

Their recovery began. My whole life has been witness to their process. There was the despair and grief of the betrayal, attempts at reconciliation interrupted by relapses. There was victimization and blame. Mom's depression that bordered on suicidal ideation. Her own dysfunction: an addiction to food and shopping to numb the pain and the inability to emotionally regulate that resulted in severe and terrifying raging. They were in and out of counseling and Twelve Step programs. Thankfully, they had the support of a handful of people who held space for them, grieved with them, and accepted them. Along the way there were terrible therapists, pastors who outed them to their congregations, friends who rejected them, and countless other challenges.

To me, this was marriage and love was struggle. It was a lot of fighting and trying, hurting and hoping. Commitment was staying, hard work, second chances. But in the end, for them, it was worth it. Now, they experience more joy and intimacy in their marriage than ever. They're emotionally available, like providing a safe place when I needed it most. They are patient and generous, acknowledging with sorrow in their eyes the shortcomings of their earlier parenting years. They are some of the bravest, most loving people I know. When I asked them to share their stories for this book, stories that so many would keep buried and silent, they looked at me and said, "You have to do it. The truth is the most powerful thing there is."

I carry both the burdens and the blessings of my ancestors in my bones. In order to understand who I am, where I come from, and why I chose what I did, I look to those who came before, to long before my story ever began.

༄

Dad was the firstborn in a family of four children. His mother, Sue, married at eighteen, right after high school. The man she chose, Will, had lost his own mother at a young age. Will traveled often for work and when he was home, kept emotional distance. My dad recalls camping trips where Will would be out fishing alone in a boat. All my dad wanted was to be out there with him, to have some sense of connection. But Will died suddenly of a heart attack at twenty-eight. My dad was ten. His youngest sibling was only nine days old when the tragedy struck. Sue began to look to my dad—the eldest—for support that escalated into an unhealthy, boundaryless reliance.

Eventually, Sue remarried a widower, Harry, who himself had four children. When Harry was a child, his father had dropped him off at an orphanage following the death of his mother. So, Harry brought his own wounds, and the father figure my dad hoped for in his new family was nowhere to be found. Dad grew severely depressed; even in a combined family of eight, he felt utterly alone. He always knew something wasn't right, but was never able to name exactly what it was.

He thought the sexual longings he experienced would go away when he got married. But the abandonment and loneliness he carried became the affliction he would later try to escape through years of sex addiction. He allowed his true self to be known for the first time in his life at the age of thirty-four. Admitting his addiction was the first step on his long healing journey.

Mom was the firstborn of three children, destined for the caretaker role in an alcoholic family. She knew exactly what she had to do to avert parental rage: be perfect, look pretty, work hard, and overachieve. Meanwhile, her own feelings and opinions were unimportant. Her parents fought so violently that once her father held a pitchfork over her mother's head. There were belt beatings and trauma from sexual abuse. All the violations slowly led to an erosion of being able to identify her own feelings or recognize red flags. She was told, "Children are to be seen and not heard," to "stop crying or I'll give you something to cry about," and "hot weather is hard on little fat girls, isn't it?"

Eighteen years into her marriage, she still didn't know how to voice her internal fears and concerns: *Why does my husband come home so late? Why does he rarely initiate sex?* Deep down, she knew something was wrong. Her discounted feelings were finally validated with Dad's confession. How could she have chosen someone who hurt her more than her own father? When she confided in her parents, they waved her off. "You just need to have a glass of wine," they said.

Resentfully, she attended Twelve Step groups, questioning why she had to work on her husband's problem. For years, she played the role of victim, ignorant of how to take responsibility for herself. She raged and blamed, emotionally volatile and reactive. Through Step work she found a safe space, finding a new way to process her wounds, take responsibility, and communicate in a healthy way. She reclaimed the power she'd sacrificed as an invisible child.

"Anything less than my husband's addiction wouldn't have turned my world upside down," she says now. "It invited me to take action, to look at myself with honesty and compassion. It was a very unwelcome gift, but it finally introduced me to myself."

Dr. Brené Brown writes in *Daring Greatly*: "When it comes to our sense of love, belonging, and worthiness, we are most radically shaped by our families of origin—what we hear, what we are told, and perhaps most importantly, how we observe our parents engaging with the world."[10]

For some of us, we could spend the rest of our lives healing the first part of our lives. For much of mine, my parents were trying to dull the wounds from deeply dysfunctional and traumatizing childhoods. They were working with what they knew and what they knew was broken to begin with. No one in my family emerged unscathed. My siblings and I were all deeply impacted and struggled with forgiveness. We harbored resentments and had much to overcome within ourselves, our relationships with them, *and* with our romantic partners.

The sad truth is that I learned to give myself away long before I ever became a wife, before I even became a woman. My childhood was the training ground. The codependent tendencies I knew so well started as a young girl where I learned to get my needs met by caretaking, pleasing, and performing, even if it meant self-sacrificing and self-abandonment.

I was enmeshed first with my mother. The attention in our home centered around her and her big emotions. If she wasn't okay, no one was. I became a confidant for her, a receptacle to hold her pain. Emotional boundaries blurred. I cared that my mom was always so sad; I wanted to help her, but a little girl isn't supposed to carry the weight of knowledge that her mother wants to drive off a cliff. A little girl doesn't know that when her mother is screaming in her face, her words like venom, the poison doesn't have anything to do with her. Being on the receiving end of her rage left its scars.

I was a teenager listening to them fight when I promised myself: *I'll never choose a partner who will betray me like Dad betrayed Mom.* But I also never healed the wounds I inherited from childhood or rewrote the stories I observed about love and relationships. I had no idea how deeply they impacted me, how *their story* informed *my story* and what I would normalize. Eventually and unconsciously, I chose the very thing I wanted to avoid. As Carl Jung famously wrote, "The psychological rule says that when an inner situation is not made conscious, it happens outside as fate."

When I fell in love with Nick and chose to marry him, I thought I'd avoided any future risk of abandonment and betrayal. I truly believed that I was in a loyal relationship that would be nothing like my parents'. In reality, I chose what I knew. I chose what had been modeled. I chose someone who, despite all the red flags, I felt comfortable with.

The role I played in childhood became the role I played in my marriage. I perpetuated the enmeshment and codependence I knew. *I accepted what I thought was normal.* In choosing Nick, my choice reflected who and where I was: *unhealed*.

Nick came from his own lineage of trauma, enmeshment, and addiction. He was the son of an addict; I was the daughter of an addict. We were wounded children who became wounded adults, the damage repeating. The ghosts of our childhoods had come out from the shadows to play.

So why did my parents' love eventually flourish while mine crumbled? *Willingness.* Dad was willing to do anything to rebuild trust; he followed his apology with action. I think back on Nick's response. His apologies felt meaningless in the wake of continuing the first affair. There was no willingness: not for therapy, not to talk about it, not even to read a book about it. He blamed his indiscretions on me, all the while saying he didn't know what he wanted. After the crash, he vowed to be a better man, but quickly slipped back into old behaviors.

At the time, I looked to my parents' story for both inspiration and hope—if my parents had done it, so could we. It is the ability to move through heartrending challenges as a couple, where both individuals choose to do so, that can make a relationship even more resilient. Either way, both people need to be there, in that space of choosing, deciding that despite the pain, the difficulty, that growing in love is possible. And with the right person, a willing person, it can be. The pivotal difference? I was doing it all alone. The writing was on the wall, but denial blinded me. I harmed myself by staying in a relationship where my partner was unwilling to change or take responsibility. What if I had waited longer? Could he have done the work? Maybe. But how many wounds can one endure under the pretense of waiting?

Lori, who stood by my side during those agonizing months, later told me, "It was like you were running away." I was. It felt like my life depended on it. If I hadn't left, would I have ever embarked on this healing journey? Perhaps just like my parents, nothing short of the affairs and divorce would have made me look at myself so honestly.

The inquiry of inheritance isn't about placing blame on the past, on parents. It's about taking responsibility for the choices made and for the future. The wounds of my family story have to be inspected and put to rest.

Mark Wolynn, author of *It Didn't Start with You*, writes: "The vast reservoir of our unconscious appears to hold not only our traumatic memories but also the unresolved traumatic experiences of our ancestors. . . . Unresolved traumas from our family history spill into successive generations, blending into our emotions, reactions, and choices in ways we never think to question."[11]

Trauma from at least three generations can manifest itself in descendants' lives. That means the unhealed pain of the mothers, fathers, grandmothers, grandfathers, great-grandmothers, and great-grandfathers can continue to be expressed in their offspring.

In *The Myth of Normal*, Dr. Gabor Maté writes, "Trauma is in most cases multigenerational. The chain of transmission goes from parent to child, stretching from the past into the future. We pass on to our offspring what we haven't resolved in ourselves."[12] The inherited and perpetuated wounds passed down through family lines can be powerful and prevailing.

When I trace the web of trauma in my family, patterns become eerily evident. Borderline personality disorder was passed down for an astounding four generations. Addiction was passed down through countless more and manifests into my family today. Marriages that began at young ages then quickly evolved into abusive relationships have been repeated over and over. As children, so many of my ancestors were not given the love, emotional intimacy, or safe attachment they deserved. Deep emotional needs went silenced, shamed, or altogether unmet. They were "seen and not heard," forced into being the parent figure themselves, told to stay small and quiet, beaten and bullied. I saw that these sad cycles would continue until someone became *aware* enough to say, "Enough!"

I have a choice: continue the patterns or break the cycles. Not only for me, but for them, and for any hope of old wounds not being projected onto new life.

In *How to Do the Work*, Dr. Nicole LePera writes: "It's our responsibility to teach ourselves the tools to meet our own needs. When we reparent, we begin by learning how to identify physical, emotional, and spiritual needs and then we practice noticing the conditioned ways we've gone about attempting to get those needs met."[13]

The process of granting oneself what was neglected or denied as a child can be a painful road riddled with land mines of grief, the kind that like to point fingers and name names. The process is about moving from the unconscious to the aware, to engage in new ways of being and doing. To create a new legacy, one free from the chains of the past. That which was denied must be granted. What was damaged must be nurtured. What was unseen must be witnessed. What was not given a voice must be spoken.

This journey into the past has helped me find grace, empathy, and understanding for myself, my parents, and all those who came before. I visualize my ancestors standing beside me now. They're cheerleaders in my blood and bones, urging me to fight for autonomy, boundaries, worth, self-respect, and freedom. Cycles can be broken. Wounds healed. The future is wide open and free.

33

FORGIVENESS

Forgiveness exists on an ever-changing spectrum where the pendulum swings from willingness to righteousness. Somewhere in the center is the ability to say "I forgive you" from a place of hurt *and* compassion. It's a difficult place to find and a harder place to stay.

There are small types of forgiving. Forgiveness for the minor infractions, the unintentional hurts, the miscommunications. The bruise will last a little while, but after enough time has passed—an hour or a day—it fades, sometimes forgotten completely. The damage inflicted was minimal, temporary, easy to overcome.

Then there are big types of forgiving. Forgiveness for the heavier blows, the actions that led down a slippery slope, the lies, the betrayal, the secrets, the things that can really damage, even destroy. With these indiscretions, the wound festers or becomes a scar. Eventually, when enough time has passed, it may not ache as it once did, but the reminder, the remnants of what was, will always be there. Big forgiveness can take months, years, a lifetime. For some, it may never come. It may be in the past, but it impacts *all of the future*; it *changes* things. Big forgiveness demands big consideration. Can trust be rebuilt? Can I move past this?

Big forgiveness isn't possible when "I'm sorry" is uttered as empty words without action. Without willingness to change there is no path to reconciliation. Sometimes we must forgive when no "sorry" is ever uttered, when the genuine apology never comes. Isn't that the hardest of all? To forgive when the one who harmed never acknowledges the full extent of the damage they inflicted, never to make amends with honest words and contrite action? Our pain and anger are justified. We are left to be our own healer, to grant *our own* freedom through forgiveness.

Caroline Myss writes in *Anatomy of the Spirit*, "By far the strongest poison to the human spirit is the inability to forgive oneself or another person. . . . Violations of the heart must be rectified, or healing will be impossible."[14]

The beautiful thing about forgiveness—real, true, authentic forgiveness—is that it dissolves the chains that tie us to the past. I've come to understand that by not forgiving, the only one I'm shackling is me.

I discover the interview by accident. While doing research for this book, I dig into the past: articles, newspapers, any media I can find. On Google, something catches my eye. I inhale sharply and click the link. I scan the description and freeze. I heard a rumor years ago that maybe there would be a deeper dive into the cause of the helicopter crash. Here it is. I listen to a sound bite in suspense. My body tense, breath shallow.

Thankfully, I'm not alone. From across the room, A. can tell something is wrong. "What's up?" he asks.

I want to throw something. Instead, I pull out my headphones and say flatly, "There's an interview."

Confused, he asks, "Who did what?"

"About the crash my ex-husband was in, there is this big interview about it. I just listened to a clip."

Concern crosses his face. He knows me well enough to know that I'm not okay. He jumps up onto the bed, wraps his arms around me, and looks at the screen.

"Do you want to hear?" I ask.

He nods. I hit play and listen to the intro again, this time with the comfort of him by my side. My body heat rises. My heart beats harder.

"That's him . . ." I explain when Nick's voice sounds.

When it ends, A. asks gently, "Are you okay?"

Unable to hold it in any longer, I shake my head and begin to cry. Hot, salty tears leak from my eyes. A. pulls me into his chest, holding me tight. A mix of emotions well up. Even after all these years, they return for what seems like the hundredth time. I don't expect A. to understand, and I can't begin to explain.

"It's okay to let it out," he tells me. "Don't hold it in." When he kisses the top of my head, I fall apart even more.

We listen to the full feature together a few days later. Interspersed throughout the entire hour and a half is Nick. I haven't heard his voice in years. Listening to him after all this time feels wrong, like I shouldn't be here, shouldn't be doing this. I'm violating some sort of barrier I put between myself and the past. I wrestle between practicing detachment and an onslaught of emotions as the story unfolds.

Every time I hear Nick's voice, I involuntarily hold my breath. Near the end, the interviewer, alluding to Nick's PTSD and survivor's guilt, asks him, "What was the lowest point?"

I grasp A.'s hand tighter. *What is he going to say?* My mind races. I can't move. My face grows hot.

"You're going to think I'm crazy . . ." Nick grows audibly emotional. Slowly, he responds, "The barrel of a gun to my head."

I tune out. Silence fills my brain like a flat lake of nothingness. Maybe it's minutes, maybe seconds. It takes time for me to come back to my body. For my breath to find itself. For my heartbeat to catch. I grow agitated. Restless. Angry.

What Nick didn't say, what he never said, was that through all of this, the lowest of the low, a loss he never mentioned, the person on the receiving end . . . *was me*. I was there. I went through hell and back with him, and for him, and when he reached that pit of despair, the barrel of a gun to his head, I was there. That small detail, *our marriage*, is completely absent. The media outlet even featured a photo I took on my phone after the crash, but as a character, I don't exist. Perhaps it has no place in Nick's recollection, in the story he prefers to tell that is easier. In the end, he's a victim. In so many ways he is; in so many ways he isn't.

In the days following the interview, my forgiveness pendulum swings to righteousness. How desperately I wish forgiving was a one-and-done deed. I'm confronted all over again with the maddening desire for vengeance. The longer I sit with the anger, the more it becomes clear: Underneath that anger is sadness. Looming mountains of sorrow and profound valleys of grief.

I decide to confront the origins of the sadness that lingers, to look back.

I'm home alone, and the house is quiet. Day has turned to night; silence settles in. I nestle into bed, plugging in an old backup drive and navigating to Nick and I's wedding album. Before clicking open, I take a deep breath. I haven't seen these photos in years.

I open the folder and browse highlights of our big day. Getting my makeup done with my bridesmaids. My sister helping me into my dress. Mom arranging flowers. The first look with Nick under a pier. To my surprise, I feel neutral. It's like I'm an observer, peering in through a window, watching from afar.

My face, my hair, a pearl necklace, a bouquet of hydrangeas and peacock feathers. I can't help but look at that girl and think, *How perfect you are.* I have so much tenderness for her, so much compassion for the things she would feel and the experiences she would have through being married. Even if I could hold her sweet, hopeful face and tell her what I know now, it wouldn't have changed a thing. The heartbreak that she would need to endure—to learn all that she did—to become who she was meant to be. She made her decisions. She had to find her way. I can forgive her for that.

The thing is, if I'd loved myself, truly loved myself, would I have ever chosen him? If I'd met my own needs by looking inward and knew that worth and belonging were an inside job, would I have ever given myself away like I did? What if I chose Nick to teach me how to choose me first?

It seems radical, this idea that Nick might be one of my greatest teachers, a teacher who made it possible for me to meet the depths of myself. Then again, love and forgiveness are the most revolutionary forces on earth. I wouldn't be here, where I am—living a life I love—without him.

What's more, as I browse the photos, I'm struck by Nick. I remember how attracted to him I was, the joy that was so evident between us on our wedding day. If I could hold his strong, persistent face and tell him what I know now, it wouldn't change a thing. He had to wander into his darkness as much as it incited mine. He had to face his shadows as much as I had to be introduced to my own. What if we did it all with our souls knowing it would bring us to our knees?

There is no villain to be found here. Nick didn't marry me intending to betray and break his vows. I believe that he believed in the man he so badly wanted to be. But intentions are not the same as accountability, and meaning well doesn't translate to acting well. It is inevitable that we will both wound and be wounded. Through feeling all of this, dredging up the past, confronting the shadows, I'm slowly but surely setting myself free. By choosing to forgive, I'm reclaiming my personal power.

I forgave when I had the vision of Nick's hands hovering over my heart. When I heard his sadness on the other end of the call as I told him our marriage was over. When I picked up the credenza and saw the gutted look on his face. When I signed the settlement papers and dropped them in the mail. I forgave when I listened to the interview and realized that he is trying to make peace with his past the best way he knows how, as am I. I forgive even now, as I dig up these wedding photos and am reminded of the sweetness we once shared.

Big forgiveness is not a one-and-done deal. Whenever therapy brings up a wound or a resentment surfaces, whenever I make a payment on our wedding debt or feel old fears that my growing relationship with A. brings, I choose to forgive again and again.

Healing is rarely linear.

Gently, I close my computer and unplug the drive. Leaning back into a wall of pillows, I place my hands on my heart. There's no racing terror, no anxiety coming to the surface. This is how I know I've come so far. That every effort I make towards reclamation matters.

Forgiveness is not absolution. It doesn't mean compromising boundaries or personal safety. Nick has no part in my life. We don't speak and it's better that way. Ultimately, I believe we will all be held accountable for our behavior—that his soul will have to reconcile with his actions—as I reconcile with mine. But I forgive to release a burden that was never meant to be permanently carried. To create a life of liberation uninhibited by old grievances and resentments.

Withholding forgiveness casts chains about the heart that only restrain. For me, there's no freedom to be found in righteousness.

Admittedly, it takes me longer to forgive the women I once called enemies. Christine, Sasha, photo girl. I learn to thank them for being part of my path, for helping me eventually meet the woman I was meant to become. I pray they be blessed.

At the end of the day, forgiveness teaches me to hold space for all that was chosen, allowed, endured, and perpetrated, on *all* sides. I forgive for him, for them, for me, for all the people in between that our lives touch. Forgiving serves as one of the most radical acts of self-love. I forgive because *I* deserve it. If there is any journey to be taken for the well-being of heart and soul, this is it. Forgiveness acts as a bridge, the one that leads us home.

34

MEDICINE

In *This Is Your Mind on Plants*, Michael Pollan writes: "We have much to learn from traditional Indigenous cultures that have made long use of psychedelics like mescaline or ayahuasca: As a rule, the substances are never used casually, but always with intention, surrounded by ritual and under the watchful eye of experienced elders."[15]

Plant medicine can also be understood as "parts work." Trauma fractures us, splinters us. The plants can help us reclaim and reunite with those wounded parts of ourselves in order to heal. My journey has led me to work with one such medicine.

The shaman leads us outside to the balcony. Her long brown hair and cinnamon skin are accentuated by the colorful ceremonial dress she's wearing. I've been working with her since she helped me navigate my breakup with Sam. After traditional therapy and other modalities, I decided I wanted a spiritual mentor who offered alternative approaches to healing. Shamans are said to work with and on behalf of the individual, the community, and the planet by serving as an intermediary between the physical and spiritual realms.

I stand with a small group of strangers, watching the sun set on the horizon, sinking into endless blue. I'm apprehensive about what lies ahead. Before coming, A. had pulled me into a tight hug. "I hope you have a beautiful experience," he'd said.

The shaman calls us forward one at a time to receive the ceremonial preparation of tobacco and Agua Florida—a flower essence from Peru. Her brown eyes meet mine and she murmurs quietly, "Blessings on your journey, Sarah." I bow my head and step back, entering ceremony. After this initiation, we'll spend the rest of the evening in silence as we work with the medicine.

We sit in a circle, eleven of us, perched on cushions in a living room with floor-to-ceiling windows overlooking waves that disappear into the twilight. Furniture has been pushed aside; an altar adorned with flowers, candles, and crystals occupies the center of our ring. I glance at the designated puke bucket next to me and feel some trepidation. The shaman seems to read my mind. "Whatever you've heard, I encourage you to let it go. Forget it. Approach this with no preconceived notions or expectations and have your own experience." After greeting the cardinal directions and a lengthy meditation, we're ready for the ceremony. One by one we sit before her to receive our portions.

I hold the paper cup to my heart; the smell of the liquid is strong and pungent, and my stomach churns. *Breathe*, I remind myself. *Just breathe through it.* We're instructed to speak to it, to declare our intentions and offer up gratitude for the opportunity to work with this sacred teacher. A murmur of soft voices sweeps through the room.

I whisper, "I'm here with an open heart and mind, and I'm so grateful to work with you. Help me find what I seek."

The shaman's voice breaks the silence, "It's time."

I stir the contents of my cup—a dark brown sludge—with a plastic spoon. I raise it to my lips; the smell intensifies. My heart rate rises. *Breathe.* I down the contents. The taste fills my mouth. Roots, earth. I feel the trail of liquid as it slides down my throat, through my chest, into my belly. *Don't throw up, don't throw up.* It occurs to me to ask the medicine for assistance. *Please*, I say to the contents in my belly, *I don't want to vomit. If that's what you have in store for me, I'll do it. But if not, please don't let that be my experience.* I surrender, close my eyes, and wait.

Sometime later, someone is retching across the circle. With their head down in a bucket, the sounds of their purge fill the room. Usually, I'd get queasy at the sight and sound of someone being sick, but for some reason, I'm unperturbed. Earlier, the shaman had said this is one of the gifts the medicine offers: deep release. Other than a gurgling in my stomach, I don't feel anything strange happening. *Maybe I didn't have enough? Maybe the medicine won't work for me? If this is the case*, I coach myself, *that's okay, just enjoy the music and make the most.* I feel some disappointment at the prospect. It's hard to shake the expectations I came with, the incredible stories I'd heard from others.

Minutes after this thought, a sensation stirs. Heat builds, then radiates up my legs. It spreads from my core, diffusing into my bloodstream, where it settles into my brain. A heaviness engulfs me completely, turning my body to cement. I know that even if I wanted to, I can no longer move. I become completely immobilized as the medicine takes hold. It's slightly terrifying, this powerlessness. *Breathe*, I remind myself, *just let go.* There's little I can do anyway. Resisting the tidal wave is impossible, so I let it sweep me away.

I close my eyes and the visions begin. Wild, dark, visceral. I'm tumbling off a cliff, descending into blackness, falling helplessly into a void. Black lilies, green vines growing out of the inky dark, wrapping me up, swallowing me. *It can get darker. I can take you to the depths*, says a voice. More images. Death. Decay. Destruction. Burning. The guidance our shaman had given us earlier comes back to me: "We always have a choice," she'd said. "The medicine shows us two things: love or what gets in the way of love. Ultimately, where you go on this experience is up to you."

I want to chart a different course. With my eyes sealed shut, I feel into the energy of the room, wondering how my friends are faring. Instead of feeling it, *I see it.* I see the energy of everyone sitting in the circle; it flows from each person and weaves between us. *What would happen*, I wonder, *if I open my eyes? Would the magic be gone or would I still see it?* I decide to try. I open my eyes and look around the dark living room.

My breath catches. The energy is still here, flowing between us, but there is so, so much more. As I think a thought, the energy of the thought takes form from my head and floats into the ether. As I direct my focus to someone in the circle, it takes the form of white lace, intricate and delicate. The lace multiplies itself from me to them, spreading across the room. The woman across the circle takes on the face of a cat. I look at the shaman. Her shape morphs as she walks around the circle: a grandmother, a pharaoh. Lines of light emanate from the man seated next to me, glowing lasers that take on geometric forms across his body as he sprouts wings and becomes a galactic warrior. *It appears I took enough medicine.* I look out the windows, up at the stars splashed across the sky. They seem to blink at me—wait no, *they're communicating.* I realize they are watching us down here, singing about us, *singing to us.* The roses in the center of the room catch my attention; *they're alive*, not just plant-alive, but alive with a spirit, an essence. A soft pink glow emanates from them, and it seems as if they, too, *are singing.* Everything is alive. Energy is flowing everywhere and the more I notice it, the more it seems to grow, happy to be acknowledged.

A veil has been lifted. I seem to glimpse into the other side with eyes wide open. Then, I'm taken to a place where I lose the capacity for language. Words no longer matter; they are so small for an experience so big. I lose myself in this realm where everything is possible, everything exists, and everything can be known.

∽

Later, the shaman offers an opportunity to receive a healing from her; unable to walk, I crawl my way through the dark.

"What can I help you with, Sarah?"

I sit back on my knees. *Breathe.* It takes a moment for me to recall how to speak; words seem foreign, feel strange in my mouth. "I'm having a hard time knowing where to go from here. I feel at a loss, overwhelmed by everything I'm seeing."

"Okay," she says, "hold still."

She places something heavy in my hands and curls my fingers around its smooth shape. Making a whooshing sound with her breath, she takes feathers and runs them along my head, my shoulders, and down my chest. When she's finished, calm radiates throughout my body. She tells me, "The message for you is to imagine yourself as a little girl. Spend time with the child inside of you. See what comes as an opportunity to love on those parts of yourself more deeply." I nod, trying to hold on to her words as I crawl back to my cushion.

A new vision comes. *No wait, this is familiar. This is a memory.* I'm a teenager sitting on the floor of the bathroom, my eyes red from crying; the loneliness and sadness are overpowering. I look in the cabinet for something that will end the agony. I don't want to feel this pain anymore. I look into the mirror and hate who I see. She's ugly, fat, unlovable. In this moment, I really think that no one would miss her if she was gone.

The memory is visceral, a sharp knife in my gut. I see myself there, huddled up and alone on the dirty floor. Suddenly, there is a knock on the door, it opens, and someone makes their way in. *It's me.* Only me as I am now. Me as the woman that I've become. This younger version looks up at me, her eyes full of admiration and awe. I feel so much compassion for her, for this hurting little girl. I kneel down next to her and take her hands into mine. I look into her red-rimmed eyes and tell her, "You're so strong. You'll get through this. This pain won't last forever. It's going to get better. You'll have a life beyond what you can even imagine, full of love and adventure and beautiful things. A life worth living a million times over."

She looks at me with longing. "I want to be just like you," she says.

"And so you will be," I say, taking her into my arms, holding her. "I love you," I whisper.

We grow into each other, our shapes morphing until we are indistinguishable, no more her, no more me . . .

My eyes are wet. The medicine, however, isn't finished with me. Another memory surfaces, a piece of the past I'd completely forgotten, buried deep within.

I'm seven years old, sitting in a room with my mom and two little brothers. We're getting ready for bed and my shirt is off. We all have rashes and my mother is applying ointment. My youngest brother, only a few years old, points to my belly. In his sweet baby voice, he asks, "Mommy, what is that? What's wrong with Sawah?"

I look down, the pudge of my soft belly spilling into three distinct rolls. Immediately, heat rises up my neck; my face turns beet red. I feel a protective instinct to cover up, embarrassed. I look down. *What is wrong with me?* For the first time in my life, I feel shame. Deep, cascading humiliation for what I see when I look down at my body. I learn a new story: *Something is wrong with me. My body is something to be ashamed about.* From that day forward I would believe I was fat and nothing could convince me otherwise.

My lips tremble as I recall the aching memory for the first time. I look down at my body, a body I have come to respect and appreciate. *It isn't true*, I tell her. *I'm sorry. I love you so much. Not just now, but then and for all you've ever been.* It's visceral; I don't only see her as beautiful, I *feel* her as beautiful. More than beautiful, she's perfect. *She's a damn goddess.*

I sit as it washes over me like a tidal wave. I feel my entire being flowing, beating, expressing itself in harmony and perfection. I'm connected to my sexuality with no reservation, what it means to be a woman—a creator of life—from a place of divinity, connected to every curve, to my mother, my sister, my grandmother, and the entire feminine presence that has ever existed with the deepest, most reverential respect.

For the first time in my life, I experience my body from a place of total acceptance, a place of overwhelming love and awe. I'm awash in the glow of a woman who is on fire with the power of her own existence. I dive deep into this feeling, wanting to soak it up and store it away forever.

But what comes next is grief. Grief that it took me so long to get here, for denying myself this awareness, this gift, this truth. For all the ways I covered up, made myself small, and denied the inherent perfection within. Grief for my mother, my sister, my grandmother, who may not experience this power and ownership in their bodies that I'm feeling now.

Tears fall from my eyes as the plant medicine brings me home to my body in a way I never imagined possible. I feel myself sinking deeply, truly, into my own skin. I wake from the sleep of limitation and imitation.

When the ceremony ends at 2:00 a.m., I sit outside on a plastic chair and wrap myself in a blanket. The air is crisp, and the sound of the waves below the bluff washes over me. Everyone else is inside, sharing about their experiences, but I need to be alone. I still feel the last remnants of the medicine and powerful emotions swirling through me.

I take in the magic of the night: the chill in the wind, the stars singing above, the clouds floating by illuminated by the moon. I gaze out at the ocean. The most profound sense of peace settles around me. I feel as if arms are wrapping me up and holding me tight, when a voice whispers: *I've got you.* A presence that can only be described as pure love infiltrates my being. I've never felt so held or experienced such trust.

I understand now. We cannot heal without involving the body. Perhaps even more than our minds, our bodies are the keepers of memory. In future ceremonies, the medicine will literally shake loose what has been suppressed in my cells as my limbs involuntarily stretch and jerk and tremble. If trauma splinters us, the plants help reunite. If my own body has been a stranger, it's time to meet her as an ally.

35

MY BODY IS MY ALLY

Both memories that surfaced during the ceremony had to do with shame. And no amount of inspirational Brené Brown quotes, motivational Tony Robbins hype, or, gasp, even crystals, can be the remedy.

Before I looked down to see my rolls when I was young, I hadn't rejected myself. That first time I felt shame was the decisive instant I attached badness, *wrongness*, to my body. After that, I longed to be different. I learned to look outside myself for standards of desirableness, rightness, enoughness. There are so many rules of *how to be* and *how not to be* a girl in this world. But when we teach little girls to be ashamed of their bodies, they become disembodied women.

I had an early education in separation. I sucked in my stomach. Wore baggy clothes. Hid the stretch marks on my inner thighs. Covered my mouth when I laughed. Hated the crow's-feet when I smiled. At thirteen, I was hiding diet books under my bed. First, the shame came for my body. Then, it came for my sexuality.

My first sexual experience was unwanted. I wasn't yet ten, but I was aware enough to know that everything about it felt wrong. Threatened and bribed, I went along with it. The shame would eat me alive from the inside out. It would take years of silent suffering for my dark secret to be revealed.

The early messages about my physical body? Embarrassment. About my sexual parts? Disgrace. The doctrine from the religion I was raised with regarding sex before marriage? Forbidden. The unspoken from my parents regarding sex? More shame. It was written all over Dad's face, it was screamed from my mother's mouth, it was alive and well deep within me. Shame was rampant.

After the plant medicine ceremony, I understand just how much of my life has been spent outside my own skin, dissociated, disconnected, at odds. In wanting my body to be something other than what she was, I never learned how to be in relationship with her. I never grasped what a healthy relationship to sexual pleasure, self-esteem, and connection to my body might look or feel like.

I become aware just how much this separation and rejection cost me. It informed the choices I made, the way I moved through the world from a place of compromised worth and personal power; it drove me to look for external validation almost everywhere, all the time, at my own expense. Did how I feel about, treat, and perceive my body inform how I allowed myself to be treated with Nick? How could it not? A part of me wonders about the ambivalent hookups I said yes to that summer after leaving him. Were the unsatisfying encounters an attempt to get my power back after having felt powerless for so long? An unconscious acting out?

I acknowledge that there is a part of me that has needed to feel wanted. At times, I had rationalized blurry boundaries and was open to receiving male attention because it felt good. When I'm honest about this pattern, the inner critic gets loud. No amount of external validation will ever be enough if something deep within is unsettled.

The damaging stories that I'd been told—and that I had told

myself for years—had been buried in my bones and needed to be extracted from the marrow. If I *learned* such harmful self-betrayal, then there must be freedom in *unlearning*. It's time to unlearn *not being* in relationship with my body, my sexuality, and ultimately, my worth. Freedom and healing are found not in silencing my inner critic, but in gently telling that part of me: *We know better.* This isn't about what others perceive of me—rather when I look in the mirror, am I enough for me? When I close my eyes, am I at home underneath my skin? I endeavor to find belonging within to be at peace without.

The moment I stop asking my body to be different is when a genuine relationship with her begins. It's an accumulation of gradual choices where I choose, again and again, that she's enough. I engage with this process over and over, every single day. Acceptance can serve as the ultimate act of reclamation after a lifetime of rejection. I wonder if it's any coincidence that the safest and healthiest I've ever felt in my body preceded the safest and healthiest romantic relationship I've ever had?

I'm still unlearning. There are so many layers. Being triggered serves as a clue, highlighting the unhealed. Much of what I judge in others is actually what I lack. What I reject is what I haven't yet found ownership of. What I project is what I haven't yet reconciled. I'm relentlessly re-nurturing my relationship with my body, and to her. Self-discipline replaces self-betrayal. Now, she and I are in this together, and that is no small thing—it's everything.

Ceremony marked the very first time I felt my body's true power. It surfaced from deep within and radiated through my entire being. The sensation exploded until I was so rooted in myself, so at home, that all the harmful stories I had ever told before were exposed. But goddess was such a foreign concept—so far from my Christian programming—the word itself was deeply uncomfortable.

I relate to Sue Monk Kidd's words in *The Dance of the Dissident Daughter*: "We've been conditioned to shrink back from the Sacred Feminine, to fear it, to think of it as sinful, even to revile it. And it would take a while for me to deprogram that reaction, to unpack the word and realize that in the end, goddess is just a word."[16]

I had uncovered something so unexpected that *goddess* was the only name I could put to it. I wish the feeling had lasted, but the memory of euphoria serves as my new standard.

Kidd says it best, "Waking to the sacredness of the female body will cause a woman to 'enter into' her body in a new way, be at home in it, honor it, nurture it, listen to it, delight in its sensual music. Such a woman conveys a formidable presence because power resides in her body."[16]

This is what I strive for. More often than not, I'm only catching glimpses of that woman from a distant shore. But I know what is possible, that she exists.

What is arrival? For me, it's the place where I feel at home within. Not asking my body to be that which she is not or to carry what's not hers. I tell her daily how much I love her, sending her gratitude for her incredible abilities. Instead of comparison, I choose to see difference as beautiful. Instead of rejection, I choose to accept. Instead of judgment, I choose to hold space for all the versions and all the moments. Arrival is when shame isn't given a voice louder than my knowing. Arrival is when I embrace the truth: that my body is and always has been my greatest ally.

36

ANSWERED PRAYERS

A. and I lie on yoga mats in a small, intimate studio. For a date, I've brought him to his first breathwork class. He lies in the corner of the room, a few feet from me, as the instructor guides us through the breathing sequence. Music with pounding bass fills the dark room as I become lost in the guided rhythms of breath.

Near the end of the session, my entire body is electric. Everything tingles. My brain shifts as vibrant colors start to dance in my mind. It's as if I can feel the energy of my body, of the music, of everyone in the room, swirling around me. No psychedelic medicine or ecstasy here, just the natural high of breathing.

As I lie with my eyes closed, a vision begins to form. Like smoke, I seem to rise out of myself. Floating above, I watch Sarah's chest rise and fall. As my awareness expands, I see A. below, lying on his mat, his eyes closed. Suddenly, some part of him seems to rise up and meet me in this ether. What I can only describe as *our spirits* greet each other like old friends, ecstatic to be reunited. At once familiar and undeniable, they exchange a knowing that is as real as my next breath. They utter the words we have not yet spoken. *I love you*, they say to one another.

After the class ends, A. and I walk to dinner, both laughing and giddy, high from so much oxygen. Without knowing anything about my experience, A. tells me, "It was like my soul left my body. It felt like I met yours in the center of the room and we exchanged . . . we exchanged a message. That sounds crazy, right?" He self-consciously looks away and I laugh out loud. We'd both experienced the exact same thing. We both know what the *knowing* was. Our souls are saying what our lips haven't yet.

On Halloween, a week after our breathwork date, A. makes us dinner. I pull up to find him in full costume: suspenders, glasses, a pencil protector, high-waisted shorts, and a tucked-in shirt. Laughing, we go to sit down, plates of roasted veggies in hand, but A. has a perplexed look on his face.

"What's up?" I ask.

"There's something I need to tell you."

"Okay . . ." I sit across from him and meet his gaze. "What's on your mind?" I ask, attempting to sound casual.

He hesitates. "There's something I've known for a while and I've struggled with holding it in. It feels like it's gotten to the point where I'm not being honest by keeping it to myself and it's important for me to speak it."

He has my full attention.

"The thing is . . ."—he pauses—"I'm just *so* in love with you."

The words sit in the air between us. Silence stretches as they sink in. Then, I cross the expanse between us and hold him tight. I find my voice and speak out loud what my heart knew was undeniable. "I love you too."

Eight months later, I sneak a glance at A. from across the cab of a 2016 Ram ProMaster cargo van. He shifts to low gear as landscaping supplies slide across the back. We both have the same question: Is this the one? As in, could this be our future home? Enamored with the idea of van life and totally naive about the implications of building out a camper ourselves, we pool our savings, and make an offer on the van.

On one of our very first dates, A. had asked me if I would ever live in a van. I laughed. It was on my vision board. Yeah, yeah, big surprise, woo-woo girl has a vision board. But the opportunity for this adventure came sooner than either of us expected. A. had signed up for a yoga teacher training course in Colombia. I planned to meet him after my annual summer program with the nonprofit to backpack together—or so we thought. A global pandemic has other ideas.

One month into lockdown, A. is out of work as a teacher when his international school shuts down as the students are recalled to their respective countries. I linger at my nonprofit for two more months, but it becomes clear that it's time for me to leave; I'm burned-out and disenchanted. I sell my furniture and move out of my apartment so we can focus on the van build. Only, neither of us have any clue what we're doing when we drive the nineteen-foot vehicle into his grandpa's driveway to begin the renovation.

Over the next two months, while COVID rages, we work seven days a week. Watching countless YouTube videos, spending hours researching and ordering products, digging through forums, and working long hours on the conversion. Our home on wheels slowly takes shape. A. learns electrical wiring while I learn how to plumb; he cuts holes in the steel for windows while I pack insulation. We prime, paint, cut, sand, sleep, repeat. Other than a squabble over a mattress, our relationship gets by largely unscathed. And when the paint dries, the flooring is laid, the lights work, the plants and crystals (of course) are placed, we look around and can hardly believe what we've constructed. Together, we built a dream, then set out on the open road to live it.

Solar powered and self-contained, we camp off-grid, avoiding crowded campsites altogether. The more isolated and wild, the better. Often, there is no cell phone service for days at a time. The cargo doors slide open to reveal sunsets over silhouetted peaks. We jump in alpine lakes, soak in natural hot springs, and hike to glaciers. I shave my legs naked on riverbanks and wash my hair with a ten-dollar weed sprayer from Home Depot. We gag as we take turns emptying our portable cassette toilet. I mean, if dumping each other's poo isn't love, what is?

When we get back to San Diego after five months of adventuring, instead of selling our beloved van, we decide to move in permanently. We live off of savings and work a few months of the year to support our lifestyle. Our sweet little home can go anywhere we want, anytime we want. It has everything we need because we need very little. Literally, very little—I downsized my entire wardrobe to fit into a cabinet the size of a gym locker. We spend our days in beautiful places, exploring, hiking, reading, and writing. Our adventures could fill an entire book, so A. wrote one (*Now Is the Time: A Van Life Road Trip* by Andrew Singer).

Van life gives me the space and time to embark on the dream I've dreamed for years: to write my own book. And to do so with a partner by my side who unequivocally supports me, *and* the process it requires.

In past relationships, where there was insecurity around certain topics, now there is intimacy. Where there had been discomfort, now there is pride. What was control is now trust. What was turbulent highs and lows is now consistency and emotional stability. There is encouragement for the inner work and growth. And when I once thought I had to go it alone, A. stands unwavering by my side. I have been given the gift of being in a relationship that *heals* my idea of what it is to be in a relationship.

For years, Saint Patrick's Day was an agonizing reminder, a trigger. First with Nick, then with Sam. As fate would have it, A. celebrates his sober anniversary that *very same date*. Both the lives we had known effectively ended in the space of one sunset to one sunrise. That day made it possible for an *us*.

How beautiful that yoga—a practice that gave me my strength and autonomy back—also led me to him. When we met in the studio, I had no inkling that the sweaty man before me would be my person, my future. Our friendship laid the foundation. But I might have missed this love altogether if it weren't for asking: *Why not?*

Our healed wounds have made us who we are; they were preparation for the love that we would ultimately share, and the partners we strive to be. And strive I do. Codependence still slinks in, projections arise, triggers get activated. I still look outward instead of inward for validation of being enough. I'm continually learning. But opening my heart has allowed me to go deeper into love, into healing, into life with all its glorious messiness.

The heart is too big and love too beautiful to refuse. This sweet love dares me to go deeper and be all of me, just as I am. When it came from the inside out, when I was enough on my own, and when my partner respected all the versions of me and the work I've done to arrive, I find myself in a safe relationship where the roots grow deep and nurture every area of my life. A partnership of mutual liberation. A. is the answer to a prayer that once passed my lips.

Love has taught me what I needed to learn; it always does. Most importantly, it found me when I stopped looking for it and started cultivating it. It came to me when I chose me, when I made the pivotal shift to belong to myself first.

Becoming has taught me that love is so much sweeter and more wonderful than I ever imagined it would be. It doesn't require me to give more than I have. It doesn't charge a price I cannot pay. It's not heavy like I thought it was. It isn't conditional, and I don't need to earn it. Love is gentle. It holds all the space I need. Love looks like the journey I've finally come to know so well.

37

THE RITUAL

Seven years ago, I changed my name and became a wife. Less than two years later, I googled: "how to file for a divorce." I paid the attorney fees and got the necessary paperwork notarized. When I received the official document in the mail months later, it was a welcome relief. Over time, I got used to saying my maiden name again, to not wearing my wedding ring, to checking the *Divorced* box. With the divorce final and my name restored, I thought that was that—time to move on and put it all behind me. I quickly learned it would take years to reconcile all that had transpired. Even now, there is a place to revisit. To my surprise, the pain that still lingers is around my wedding ceremony.

I'd dreamt of getting married for as long as I could remember. As a little girl, I fantasized about every detail of the big day. Buried within the loss of this dream is a place of sadness. Sad that the day I had imagined my entire life was ultimately with a man who broke our vows in every possible way, that the commitment I always believed I would only make once was shattered. That still, years later, the idea of marriage feels tainted, that dream dissolved, and all I have to show for it is a piece of paper.

An official document from the state doesn't sever the sacred vows that I committed to in my mind, body, and soul. Words have power, especially vows spoken with intention and consecrated by witnesses. Only I can release myself from their authority. I left a piece of me on a California beach one day in February, waiting and waiting for a promise that would never come true.

Esther Perel, a renowned psychotherapist, writes in *The State of Affairs*: "Just as we have marriage ceremonies to mark the beginning of a union, we also need rituals to mark the end. . . . Rituals facilitate transitions. They also honor what was."[17]

My divorce process isn't complete. The time has come to break my commitment, to release all attachments to that day, to cleanse the memories from that beach, and ease the deep ache of all that I thought my marriage would be.

I revisit the very place almost seven years to the day, the same beach where I promised *forever*. Once again, my bare feet push down into the soft, cool sand. The emerald waves of the Pacific Ocean tug at the shoreline. The sun sinks into the west, lighting up the sky as I walk the same walk I did years before. But this time, there is no groom waiting for me. No officiant who will proclaim me a wife. No fanfare, no crowd. Only my parents accompany me to the place where this journey began. It feels fitting to share this moment with them. These beautiful people who have witnessed it all: from my first breath, to giving me away, to welcoming me home, their arms always open.

I scatter white roses on the sand—white for purification, roses for love—an offering. Kneeling down, I pull out the items for my self-made ritual: the wedding vows Nick and I exchanged and a lighter. I've decided to burn them as a symbol of closure. When I bring the flame to the ink-scratched paper, I watch the smoke rise. Our words, our promises, they glow bright, then black, then turn to ash. Nothing more than smoke in the wind.

My parents stand beside me. Even if they don't always understand the woman before them—the one who's shirked her religion for yoga and crystals and plant medicine—they are unwavering. They lean in to hear me speak over the waves in the background as I slowly read the words I've written:

"I honor this sacred ground and release all negative emotion, memory, and attachment associated with my wedding. I honor and acknowledge my parents and all our ancestors who bear witness. I invite them to benefit from any and all healing taking place.

"With this ritual, I release myself from the marriage vows that were exchanged. I dissolve all obligation, responsibility, promise, and commitment. I call back my power and integrate total freedom, sovereignty, and agency of my life, heart, body, and spirit.

"I now release any energetic, karmic, soul, emotional, mental, or physical attachment from Nick. I welcome the power of grace to integrate all the lessons and gifts from our marriage. That part of my life is now finished and complete.

"With this ritual, I vow to love, honor, and trust myself for all the days of my life. I affirm and claim my innate worth on every level. I embrace this beautiful process of becoming, now and forevermore. And so it is."

I take another deep breath as I close my eyes and seal in this moment. The salty air. The breeze. The sound of the gulls. My parents embracing me. Dad has tears in his eyes when he says, "I didn't know how much we needed this too."

I see it now, how healing makes waves. How every act of reclamation generates ripples that echo far beyond ourselves. How are we to know how far the wave will travel or who will be touched by its impact?

My mother gives me one of Nana's rings, a symbol of my new commitment. I would have loved to have her here, but her body and mind are fading. She lives in an assisted care facility, and we're cleaning out her house for the realtor. Still, I feel her with me. The Troops won't ever laugh and explore and flirt shamelessly like we did, but I believe that we never truly lose the people we love.

I make my way to the shoreline where cold water swirls around my ankles as I release the ashes of my vows. Goose bumps crisscross my arms as the ocean carries away the residue of the past. I say a prayer of gratitude as the sun makes her final descent, marking the end of a day and the end of an era where old promises held power over me.

Later that night, under the watch of the full moon, I burn all the remaining letters Nick and I had ever exchanged. There are almost a hundred of them—dreams, confessions, promises. Pages-long, small notes, Post-its, journal entries, old photographs with notations on the back. From the very first to the very last, up in smoke. I feed them into the flames where they quickly turn to ash. As they burn, I grow lighter and lighter.

When the flames die, I gaze up at the full moon and whisper quietly to the Universe, "Thank you. I've never felt more grateful to be alive." How can I explain that my life has turned out more miraculous and magnificent than I ever could have dreamed? That somehow the same girl who said "I do" on the beach, who found herself on the living room floor clutching a gun, who finally said "I don't" and packed her car and left, who hiked and healed and loved again, who fumbled and finally found her way . . . I am with her. I am her. I'm the woman praying for that girl, in all her versions, through all her moments.

It took me seven years and the revisiting of painful places to come to the realization that I needed to reclaim. In truth, it doesn't matter if it takes a lifetime. Maybe I always knew one day I would arrive here. I'd kept the old letters so that when I was ready, I could honor and release all that was. This ritual restored pieces of me that had been held as ransom in the past.

What if it was always about watching it burn in order to become? Maybe all that is released today floats up and away, through time and space, back to a girl about to give her heart away. Perhaps the words in the breeze feel familiar as the whispered prayers of her future self wrap around her. She doesn't know it yet, but she's more loved by herself in that moment than a million vows made from another. All I know is that I've never felt more powerful than when I let it all go. Just me and those ashes under the watch of the full moon. I have finally learned that the vow to myself is the one that matters the most.

38

THE JOURNEY

I look at the life I have built. The love I have chosen. The journey I have taken to arrive. I remember it all and I ask myself: *Was it worth it to become?*

With clear eyes, an open, aching, brave, beautiful, bursting heart, the answer is *yes, and yes, and yes.*

It always is. It always was. Every single moment and every single choice led to the here and now.

I didn't know it at the time, but the dark that I found myself in when everything came undone was my gestation, the incubation before my rebirth, the place of breaking in order to become. I cursed it. I hated it. I couldn't imagine that one day I would say it has been the biggest gift of all, that I would call it sacred. It was a place of transformation. My baptism by fire. I had to learn: *Could I be enough for myself?* The darkness taught me things that never would have surfaced in the light.

Undoing offers the precious opportunity to rebuild. I discovered there is no freedom without responsibility. That love begins within and doesn't require self-abandonment. Ever. I rewrote my story about love. I chose a new way when I chose me first. Each and every wound has been made holy through the transformation. It was all about walking back, opening that door, wrapping my arms around us, and reuniting. It was all about becoming more powerful, true, and whole. It was all about reclamation.

Only we are responsible for who we decide to be, not in spite of the wounds, but made more beautiful because of them. Love and suffering are universal, but the power of choice is everything. This is the power of owning the story: It no longer owns me.

This is not the sad tale of a failed marriage, or the tragic saga of a helicopter that fell out of the sky and stole precious people away. It's the story of how I came to be. How I was able to love and forgive and heal from the inside out to create a wild and beautiful life where I am free. The process of revisiting and reconciling has been terrifying and transformative, rage-inducing and revolutionary. Through it all, the truth has been laid bare to honor the moments where I was reborn. Once I ventured into the Elysian Fields of my own truth and power, there was no returning to a world so small that it no longer contained my expansion. This wasn't just any journey, it was *the journey*, the most important one I could ever take.

I didn't know that when we held our hands over each other in the yoga teacher training that we were imitating energy healing. Never in my distant dreams did I imagine that years later, I would become a Reiki Master. Or that when Mimi shared her psychic message it would send me down a path of cultivating my own intuitive gifts, and that one day I would channel insights for others. That instead of self-consciously stepping onto my yoga mat, I would be confidently leading classes. All the things that helped me reclaim pieces of myself along the way have become my offering.

Home becomes the secure foundation I have built within myself. Not somewhere. Not someone. Not something. It is a place where the well runs deep, where darkness is a gift instead of a curse. Worth is nurtured from within and there is pride in the becoming. Home is when I get still, listen to the voice of my soul, and choose to belong to her first.

Like the moon, healing happens in phases. There are times when all is veiled, the world goes dark, and the way is shadowed. In these desperate moments, the stars shine brighter, offering hope. But the moon always returns, illuminating with her glow, revealing the path ahead. This is the cycle, the alchemy of life. Waxing and waning, dimming and shining. Always transforming, always where things are dying and being born again. The moon doesn't mind; she doesn't resist. She knows who she is and she goes about her work just the same.

Healing is like that: gradual becomings and steady diminishings. Cycles of endings and beginnings, iterations of deaths and rebirths. Just as the moon's radiance is the result of all her phases, so, too, is ours.

I remember a time when a hurting girl with dusty boots looked to a waterfall to inspire her how to be. By the light of the moon, she committed to taking the healing path wherever it would lead. She ventured into the wilderness, searching deep and far and wide. Slowly, she found her way after enduring, becoming the keeper of her own fire. Her rekindled spirit is wild, unapologetic, and fierce. She's so powerful in her knowing that she cannot be contained, a mass of force that belongs to no one but herself. She's unique and totally her own. Where the ashes of a life once stood, she planted her own Garden of Eden. I celebrate that girl who leaves me breathless in her glow. Because of her bravery, I have come home.

EPILOGUE

Ten years after I hiked the Grand Canyon—almost to the day—I stand atop the South Rim once again. The sun has just risen, first light reflecting off towering orange cliffs that descend seemingly endlessly into the canyon's shadowy depths. The morning sky is cobalt blue, and the scent of juniper fills the air. I shoulder my backpack. A. pulls me in tight, says a prayer, kisses me goodbye, and I am on my way. I descend the same trail, take in the same awe-inspiring vistas. While the scenery is unchanged, I am returning a very different woman.

As I hike at age thirty-three—this time with poles and knee braces—each step gives me the opportunity to reflect on how much I've changed during the time in between. Time that has seen this girl move through heartbreak and healing, to find love, let go of everything "traditional," and create a life of freedom and adventure. Time in which that girl has found the courage to write this story.

I undertook this book as a commitment to self-discipline and as an act of self-love. To honor the desire that has always been in my heart by writing something that brought me peace, clarity, and closure. Writing required me to ask the hardest questions I've ever asked myself and to get honest about it all. When I finally held the printed manuscript in my hands, something inside of me cracked wide open. I locked myself in the bathroom and fell to my knees as fat tears rolled down my face. Those tears spoke of seven years of pain and healing, of transformation and becoming. When I found the strength to stand and look at my reflection in the mirror, pride and love stared back.

In so many ways, this journey started on the road, the day I packed my car and left a life behind. Years later, the road became the place I would write. This book came into form as I typed from a camp chair overlooking deserts and lakes, mountains and valleys. I typed nestled inside Rudy, the nineteen-foot RAM ProMaster cargo van that A. and I still call home. We wrote side by side for four years, telling our respective tales, seeing the world, and falling more in love.

Six months before today's hike, A. pulled me out of the van for sunset in the middle of the Utah desert. Surrounded by towering buttes, red rock and sagebrush, he got down on one knee. There was no ring (he'd hate to pick one out I wouldn't like), no photographer, no candles, no roses. I was braless and in sweats. But it was perfect. The sky was on fire and Rudy was our only witness. It was perfect because nothing else would have been more fitting for the life we lead and the love we share. It was perfect because my entire being said a big, fat, resounding *YES*. He picked me up and we held each other tight as I cried. We stayed like that for a long time. I could tell you I was so emotional because it was such a sweet, tender moment. I could tell you it was because I felt so much love. I could tell you it was healing for me, to commit to someone like him. Someone who holds my heart as it deserves. And while it was all those things, I also said yes because even a lifetime with A. still doesn't seem like enough.

We eloped two weeks later in a sweet, simple ceremony. Of all the adventures, this love is the best one by far.

A. is back at the van. I wanted to hike the Grand Canyon alone. To do it for me. For that girl. For this journey. For the time in between. Seventeen miles, 10,000 feet of climbing and descending, eight long hours. I jump in the Colorado River at the bottom of the canyon, the water like a baptism. I sing my way up the switchbacks. I marvel. I smile, even when the inclines kick my ass and rub my blisters raw. With two grueling miles to go, I round what must be the hundredth switchback, and there he is. A. is waiting for me, his company the sweetest, welcome surprise for the final stretch. He even quotes my own words back to me: "Sometimes it's nice to not go it alone. Even if we know that we can."

Together, we climb the last ridge. I kiss my husband and celebrate this journey—a far sweeter one than that girl of ten years ago could have ever dreamed.

A BLESSING

May our journeys lead us to face the fire of our own becoming.

May we venture into the darkness, and instead of letting it define us, let it generate rebirth.

May we be cracked open and broken apart to be sculpted into something more of ourselves, to arrive more fully into our hearts and skin.

May we step into our power, into the fullest, fiercest, wildest, and most magnificent version of ourselves. May doing so blaze the path for others.

May we feel the support of those who have come before us, who stand beside us, and for those who will come after us.

May we take this journey for them, for ourselves, and for the love of all things good and true and beautiful.

May every breath remind us of the choice, the invitation that is waiting. Reclamation is the reward.

Like the moon, we become again and again along the way.

SOURCES

1. Beattie, Melody. *Codependent No More: How to Stop Controlling Others and Start Caring for Yourself.* First Spiegel & Grau edition. New York, Spiegel & Grau, 2022. Pages 76, 165.

2. Estés, Clarissa Pinkola. *Women Who Run With the Wolves: Myths and Stories of the Wild Woman Archetype.* New York, Ballantine Books, 1992. Page 153.

3. Van der Kolk, Bessel A. *The Body Keeps the Score: Brain, Mind, and Body in the Healing of Trauma.* New York, Penguin Books, 2015. Pages 81, 212, 298.

4. Eger, Edith Eva. *The Gift: 12 Lessons to Save Your Life.* New York, Scribner. 2020. Pages 11,12,16.

5. Brown, Brené. *The Gifts of Imperfection: Let Go of Who You Think You're Supposed to Be and Embrace Who You Are.* Center City, Minnesota, Hazelden, 2010. Page 87.

6. Krakauer, Jon. *Missoula: Rape and the Justice System in a College Town.* New York, Doubleday, 2015. Page 254.

7. Tjaden and Thoennes: *Prevalence, Incident & Consequences of Violence Against Women: Findings from the National Violence Against Women Survey.* November, 2000.

8 Doyle, Glennon. *Untamed*. New York, The Dial Press, 2020. Page 262.

9 Gibson, Lindsay C. *Adult Children of Emotionally Immature Parents: How to Heal From Distant, Rejecting, or Self-involved Parents*. Oakland, California, New Harbinger Publications, Inc, 2015. Pages 91, 116, 121.

10 Brown, Brené. *Daring Greatly: How the Courage to Be Vulnerable Transforms the Way We Live, Love, Parent, and Lead*. New York, Gotham Books, 2012. Page 217.

11 Wolynn, Mark. *It Didn't Start With You: How Inherited Family Trauma Shapes Who We Are and How to End the Cycle*. New York, Viking, 2016. Pages 55, 58.

12 Maté, Gabor, and Daniel Maté. *The Myth of Normal: Trauma, Illness & Healing in a Toxic Culture*. New York, Avery, an imprint of Penguin Random House, 2022. Page 34.

13 LePera, Nicole. *How to Do the Work: Recognize Your Patterns, Heal From Your Past, and Create Your Self*. New York, Harper Wave, an imprint of Harper Collins Publishers, 2021. Page 210

14 Myss, Caroline. *Anatomy of the Spirit: The Seven Stages of Power and Healing*. New York, Harmony Books, an imprint of the Crown Publishing Group, 1997. Pages 84, 85.

15 Pollan, Michael. *This Is Your Mind On Plants*. New York, Penguin Press, 2021. Page 11.

16 Kidd, Sue Monk. *The Dance of the Dissident Daughter: A Woman's Journey From Christian Tradition to the Sacred Feminine.* San Francisco, California, Harper San Francisco, 1996. Pages 72, 161.

17 Perel, Esther. *The State of Affairs: Rethinking Infidelity.* New York, Harper, an imprint of HarperCollins Publishers, 2017. Pages 285, 286.

GRATITUDE

This book is a testament to the transformative power of love in my life. It is—deservingly so—dedicated to the beautiful people who sheltered me through my darkest days.

Thank you, Max and Trina, for being such generous friends and for showing up when I needed to be shown love the most. Daryn and Cat, I cherish the time we had and the way you both took me under your sisterly wings. Lori and family, you took me in as one of your own, thank you for the home away from home. B, thank you for standing by my side through it all. E—my forever accomplice—for always being there, for your encouragement, and edits; you're etched into my heart.

Aaron, the most magnificent of older brothers, thank you for trusting I would find my way and for your thoughtfulness. To my brave, beautiful big sister, for setting the best example of the kind of woman I wanted to be; I inherited some of the best parts of me straight from you. Emma, thank you for being this books cheerleader, I'm so grateful for our sisterhood. To Michael and Joey: SMJ forever. To my other siblings, thank you for your support and for opening up your hearts again when I asked you to. You're a wild bunch; I love you all.

Mom and Dad, your love is the anchor that saved me. Under your mast, you brought me back to life. Your courage, generosity, and unconditional love inspire me. Thank you for being a safe place. There will never be enough time (or words) to express how much you mean to me.

Terry, my earth angel! From the beautiful altars holding the intention for this book, to your prayers, support, and faith; you've been instrumental on this path of sharing my story and speaking my truth. Thank you; I adore you.

A., my best friend and partner in every way; from idea, to first draft, to version after version, your insights and edits pushed me to be a better writer and to make this book what it is. Penning our stories together in Rudy the last several years—from woods to mountains to desert—has been one of the sweetest and most rewarding experiences of my life. Thank you for making not only these pages, but this adventure of love so spectacular.

To all those who helped me along the healing path: teachers, therapists, fellow authors, Parminder, and to the immeasurable gift of plant medicine; thank you for helping me come home and to know what that means from the inside out.

My early draft readers, thank you so much for your time, feedback, and support. To the professionals: Tatiana, for your copy edits. Denise, your legal expertise was invaluable. Eric McKinney at Wonderland Studios, it was a pleasure recording the audiobook with you—rock on. To the team at Books Forward, thank you so much for championing this book and elevating it in ways I never could alone. Addison, thank you for guiding me through this process with patience and care. Brooke Warner, you're a treasure trove of wisdom and a fearless trailblazer. Thank you for creating the space at She Writes Press where authors like me have a chance, for taking that chance on me, and elevating the words of women with tales to tell. To my sisters at SWP, witnessing your bravery and being a part of this community has been a pleasure; you are all inspiring.

And finally, my deepest gratitude to you, dear reader. I consider it the ultimate honor that you have spent these pages with me. Thank you, from the bottom of my heart, for taking this journey with me.

ABOUT THE AUTHOR

photo credit: Peter Heirendt

Sarah May is a yoga instructor, Reiki healer, and intuitive. She provides her clients with powerful practices and healing insights from the studio to private sessions, retreats, and women's circles. Sarah received her Master of Science in Conflict Analysis and Resolution and previously managed a non-profit. *She Journeys* is her debut memoir. In 2020, she and her husband—fellow author Andrew Singer—converted a cargo van and hit the road. They spend their time exploring and writing across America's public lands. When not on wheels, Houston and San Diego are home base.

Looking for your next great read?

We can help!

Visit www.shewritespress.com/next-read
or scan the QR code below for a list
of our recommended titles.

She Writes Press is an award-winning
independent publishing company founded to
serve women writers everywhere.